THE PUB LANDLORD'S
BOOK OF BRITISH COMMON SENSE

HODDER &
STOUGHTON

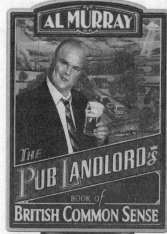

First published in Great Britain in 2007 by Hodder & Stoughton
An Hachette Livre UK company

First published in paperback in 2008

1

Copyright © Al Murray 2007

A CIP catalogue record for this title is available from the British Library.
Not the French Library.

ISBN 978 1 444 70410 5

Typeset and layout by Craig Burgess.

Printed and bound in Great Britain by CPI Mackays, Chatham ME5 8TD.

Hodder & Stoughton policy is to use papers that are natural, renewable and
recyclable products and made from wood grown in sustainable forests.
The logging and manufacturing processes are expected to conform to the
environmental regulations of the country of origin. Bla bla bla bla,
I've planted a tree, bla bla bla.

Hodder & Stoughton Ltd
A division of Hodder Headline
338 Euston Road
London NW1 3BH
Great Britain
Somewhere off the coast of Europe but not part of it

Nerds! Find out about other books at:

www.hodder.co.uk

INTRODUCTION

Welcome, and congratulations on your purchase.[1] You are now the proud owner of *The Pub Landlord's Book of British Common Sense*; and a new day is dawning in your life. For too long now Common Sense has been buried beneath a steaming heap of waffle, so-called expertise, as dished out by surveys, scientists, opinion makers, graduates, politicians, journalists and other assorted idiots.

Their combined Bad Thinking includes:
1) the belief that no one should win in running races at school in case anyone gets upset
2) the idea that owning a house in France is a decent way to spend your money
3) the belief that if your kids are naughty they are somehow sick
4) the notion that we should all talk about our feelings and that would make things better
5) the idea that we should all have carrots in our packed lunches
6) speed cameras
7) mineral water
8) hummus
9) surveys
10) and the concept that pubs are retail space, not places for people to go to and drink their worries away
11) the fact that everyone reckons they've got asthma
12) the idea that you need to drive your kids to school so they won't be run over by the people driving their kids to school

---

[1] Unless of course you've shoplifted this. Shame On You!

It is time for us to let the sweet light of British Common Sense shine through this mire of nonsense and show us the way. Common Sense is not something you learn in university. No, Common Sense is the preserve of the Common Man, and this book has been written in that spirit.

The contents of this book haven't just been thrown together – oh no – what you have here in your hands is the wisdom of ages, handed down through the centuries, amassed from the collective drinking minds of generations of decent, down to earth, normal, law abiding, hard working, decent, honest, reasonable, sensible, normal, law abiding, tax paying(ish), normal, hardworking, honourable, decent, reasonable people, normal, British people, who don't want to pay their speeding fines.

COMMON SENSE IS NOT AS GOOD AS IT USED TO BE, NOR IS IT COMMON ENOUGH.

Time was when Common Sense solutions were all around us:
'Mummy, I've been stung by a nettle!'
'Well, son, where there are nettles, a dock leaf is never far away. It's nature's medicine.'
Nowadays that exchange would run as follows:
'Mummy, I've been stung by a nettle!'
'Well, we'll sue the council for letting nettles grow in the park then!'

WITHOUT COMMON SENSE WE ARE LOST! BUT WHAT IS COMMON SENSE?

It's the sixth sense, the other five being: hearing, seeing, smelling, tasting and touching. Hearing your mate say 'do you fancy a pint?', seeing a pub, smelling the noxious yet welcoming atmosphere of the snug bar, tasting the Beautiful British Pint, and touching your mate for a fiver. Common Sense is the sense that takes care of everything else. It makes sure that you don't knock over the pint belonging to the skinhead sat on his own by the door with a pit bull that looks like him – or is it the other way round? It makes sure that (usually) you don't drink so much that you pass out with your forehead resting against the toilet cistern leaving an imprint of the words 'Armitage Shanks' embedded in reverse just above your eyebrow.

Most of all, though, it makes sure that when you open your mouth to join in a pub conversation, you don't leave yourself open to derision and scorn. Now, if you don't know what you think about a particular subject, one quick fix is to mouth off about it in the pub. Either someone will put you straight, in which case problem solved, or else some bloke will agree with you, and then you simply have to decide whether you want to be that sort of bloke, which is a straight judgement call. In just a few minutes of harmless drunken banter (unless it kicks off) you've broken the problem down to manageable proportions. The beauty of this book is that it will get you to that point without the bit where everyone looks at you and thinks you're an arse. Got that?[2] OK. Now it's time to look into what exactly Common Sense consists of.

Common Sense comprises three component parts:

Knowledge is not in itself a good thing, which is why this book isn't one of those *What To Do If Your Car Lands In A River* Type Books, which are plainly stupid and useless and too big to fit in your top pocket so pretty much unlikely to be on your person when you do career into a river.[3]

[2] Keep up!
[3] See *WHAT TO DO IF YOUR CAR FALLS INTO A RIVER*. Not that the sheer impracticality of these books stopped anyone buying them in vast amounts, it's just it only dawns on you when you get the bloody book home.

No, what Knowledge is good for, is the noble and gentle art of pub conversation. The ability to hold your own in a pub with a sprinkling of the odd pertinent fact or two is what Herberts would call a 'valuable life skill'. Handy, I'd call it. And that's the Common Sense way to put it. Read this and the quality of your pub conversations will soar, though I cannot offer a money back guarantee of any kind. And not only that, Knowledge will improve your chances in a pub quiz, and we all want to win that frozen chicken don't we? Remember, you will have far greater authority in any pub conversation if you're known as the brainy one.

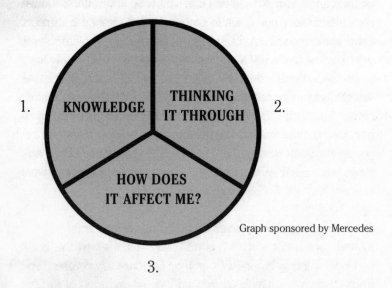

1. KNOWLEDGE

THINKING IT THROUGH   2.

HOW DOES IT AFFECT ME?

Graph sponsored by Mercedes

3.

Thinking It Through is a key component of Common Sense: by the simple application of logic – often booze fuelled – you can get to the nuggety heart of a problem quite quickly. Thinking It Through is an art – and you will see many examples of it in this book. I will explain how to spot if your pub is actually a winebar, why hanging should be brought back if only for the sake of the rope industry, and why several supposedly wise sayings from the likes of Isaac Newton and Jean Paul Sartre need to be brought down a peg or two by the application of Thinking It Through.

Finally we come to the third principle of Common Sense – **How Does It Affect Me?** This principle is best illustrated by the way people react to a Budget. Basically the Chancellor of the Exchequer can do whatever he likes, sneak through extra stamp duty, slap VAT on having children, fine airlines all he likes, as long as he leaves alone fags, booze and petrol, which are commonly known as The Things That Affect Me. Once you have a firm grip on what The Things That Affect Me are, you will begin to view the world in a new light.

So, enjoy the book – this blast of fresh air from the Mighty Trumpet Of Common Sense – and learn from it if you can. The way I see it, I've done my bit by writing it, and by reading it, you're doing yours (and your monies are gratefully received and headed straight to the carvery fund). Between us we can turn this country round and halt the tide of nonsense, cobblers and balls that we're all drowning in.

THE WAY THINGS ARE

No.1: Left-handedness Is Not Normal

Like the way that there's nothing wrong with being left-handed, nothing wrong with it at all – it's just...you're weird!! How do you do it? You're probably reading this left-handed right now aren't you? Stop it, stop it stop it – you're giving me the creeps. Alright, live and let live – you've got your left-handed scissors and whatever else, but they don't make left-handed toilet paper, do they? Your behind was made to be wiped from the right, it's a fact! Proof!! It's the way things are.

THE HONOURABLE ORDER
OF PUBLICANS
(A note about your author's professional heritage)

To be a publican is an ancient and noble calling: 'To Serve Is To Live, To Live Is To Serve', that would be our motto if we had time for one in between changing barrels and trying to get the Sky box to work. Needless to say, if we did have a motto it would be in Latin like a proper one: 'Servibus livibus, livibus servibus,' something like that. Even though the Romans are long gone a proper Latin motto is class (though when you stop to consider that the Romans were Italian it can make your head spin).

But mottos and over-achieving Italians aside, the thing about Landlords that maybe isn't obvious at first glance, supping his pint and minding his own business, is that we are the caretakers of tradition, the keepers of humanity's flame, the constant thread that runs through all human endeavour – in other words, **We Walk With History.** Oh yeah. That may seem to be a grand claim, but you know what, think again dear reader/listener (if this is the talking book, watch out for that lorry). You may think of us as the bloke stood there pretending to clean a glass with a tea towel to make it look like we're busy, but in that case you will have sadly underestimated the Brethren. For that is what we are, a Brethren, made up of Brethers (is that right?) and our line stretches back to the very dawn of time.[4]

[4] And before we get into this the Brethren includes Sistren now though I want it to be on record in the strongest of terms that I voted against that and in favour of tradition.

Forget your Knights Templar and all that Da Vinci nonsense. Forget the Masons, who are very much the new kids on the block with all their gimmicky rolled-up trouser legs and aprons. (After one of their 'top secret' meetings where do they go? THE PUB – ha ha, we win! We know it's them because they all come in looking slightly self-conscious about their creased trousers, and the only other time we see most of them is if a proper fight kicks off and they turn up with the sirens blazing and act like I don't know who they all are.) The truth is, the **Honourable Order of Publicans** have been there, in the background, pretending to clean glasses with tea towels since man first clambered down from the branches, sauntered over from where the trees were and into the pub, all the while flicking Vs at the stone age estate agent trying to sell him a cave.

As mankind developed through the Stone Age, then the Bronze Age, then the Iron Age, and most recently the Horse Brass Age, the tools required to make the perfect pub were slowly gathered together, as man and his great comforter, his constant companion, his faithful staff and crutch, soother and tormentor; booze, made their march through history, side by side. And who was pouring the booze? That's right, Us. When they finished Stonehenge where did they celebrate? Down the pub. It may just have been two big upright slabs of rock, with another one on the top, like a gigantic outdoor fireplace,

If it's a slow afternoon in the pub, why not make your own Stonehenge?

but it did the job. And let's make one thing clear right now, Stonehenge wasn't a hard hat site was it? No, because bronze age man may have been many things, but he wasn't some soft-handed twat hoping to get clocked on the head and claim the compensation.

Take for another instance the Pyramids, in ancient Egypt, best viewed as a giant game of limestone Jenga that got wildly out of hand. Even though these weren't built by the British, there's no way on God's sweet Earth that those things were knocked up without someone slaking their hard-earned thirst in some hostelry next to the Nile. After a long day's lugging giant slabs to build a  giant pointless coffin holder, the soothing words 'All right, squire, what are you having?' would make the whipping injuries fade and the thought of doing it all again tomorrow in searing 100 degree heat (it was Fahrenheit in those days, which is hotter) seem not so bad after all.

The Last Supper: no doubt there was someone there pouring the wine and serving the bread (making money on the food too, no doubt, that's the way to do it, mate, he'd have made even more if it had been Tex Mex). And even as Jesus himself was folding his napkin to one side, wiping the breadcrumbs out of his beard, and getting ready to say goodbye to the disciples, a Publican was stood somewhere in the dim background giving Judas that 'Why are you so flush, eh? You're up to something, aren't you mate?' look.

And so it goes, throughout history there has always been one of Us there, ready to offer counsel, succour and strength, as well as a

8

The Last Supper: basically a stag do, however Jesus was going to die the next day not get married, though to a man's friends it's much the same thing.

range of bar snacks and refreshing booze. The Knights of the Round Table were chivalric heroes, so you can bet they got their round in. Got their Round in, put it on the Table, hence the Knights of the Round Table – the clue's in the name. There, in a maroon doublet and hose,[5] was surely an Arthurian Guv'nor, serving vast flagons of mead to thirsty knights at Camelot. The Holy Grail was found because of the lowly ale, then filled up with the lowly ale, then passed around and kicked around the car park and lost all over again.

And what about old **Henry VIII**, eh? As he tossed another half-eaten chicken leg over his shoulder and killed yet another wife (not with the chicken leg, relax, he was bad but not that bad), he must have developed a

Henry VIII: He's wearing a sofa, look.

[5] Have you ever tried squeezing your legs into a hose? Those lads were hard as nails. Little idea what a doublet might be.

9

thirst, and where there's a thirst, there's a Publican. Although it would no doubt have been a high risk job working with the Giant Ginger Decapitator, someone had to step forward, and it would have been one of Us. And he'd have made sure there was Greensleeves on the juke box.

As the Titanic slid slowly into the icy deep, oh yes the band played on, but only because they'd had a drink or two to fortify them, and it was of course one of Us who wet the whistles of the band that played on, but did We get in the film? No. But nevertheless, We Walk With History.

After all, it is not for Us to push ourselves forward and claim the limelight. We are but humble publicans, so we have seen geniuses come and go, and great men drink themselves greater. Churchill (see CHURCHILL) single-handedly sustained several breweries through his own personal intake during the Great Depression. We have seen Empires rise and crumble, nations rise and fall, but as long as there's a Public, they will need a House, and as long as there's Public Houses, there will be Publicans. So next time you look over and see one of Us rubbing a glass like he's acting busy, and think 'Look at that lazy useless sod!' – think again.

We Live To Serve, We Serve To Live

As you read this book you will come to appreciate the sage wisdom handed down over many centuries, plus some stuff learned from pub quizzes, and quite a lot of things learned, digested and remembered under the influence of booze.

How The Start Of This Book Would Look If The Germans Had Won The Second World War

Just in case any of you were wondering:

Sie sind jetzt der stolze Inhaber des Buches des Publikation Hauswirts des britischen gesunden Menschenverstands. Es sei denn selbstverständlich Sie dieses shoplisted, Schande auf Ihnen!; und ein neuer Tag dämmert in Ihrem Leben, in einer Weise, die dieses der erste Tag des Restes Ihres Lebens ist. Für zu langen gesunden Menschenverstand ist unter einem dämpfenden Haufen der Waffel, der sogenannten Sachkenntnis, der Übersichten, der Wissenschaftler, Meinungsbilder, der Absolvent, der Politiker, der Journalisten und anderer sortierter Idioten, gesunder Menschenverstand ist gewesen oben gegen unnachgiebigen Angriff von den Gleichen des Wächters, Führung 4, bevölkert Rest von den Sechzigern, von den Lektoren und von den gobby Chefs begraben worden, die auf Ihnen Karotten in Ihrem verpackten Mittagessen essend bestehen, und es ist Zeit für mich und Sie, zu seiner Rettung zu kommen.

See, you don't like it do you?

DOCTOR SAMUEL JOHNSON (1709-1784)

Poet, essayist and lexicographer, said

*'When a man is tired of London,
he is tired of life'*

No. Dr Johnson, you see, got things all out of proportion, on account of having devoted his entire working life to producing the first ever A to Z, and this affected his ability to Think Things Through. It seems to me, an humble publican as opposed to the most celebrated wordsmith of a generation, that when a man is tired of London, he is tired of London. That same man, it seems to me, can move out of London, go and live in Los Angeles, become a famous film star, and live the life of bloody Riley, bedding starlets and snorting crack cocaine off the marbled surface of his very own personal poolside bar. Or am I missing something?

HAVE YOU GOT BRITISH THINKING?

British Thinking is the finest bloody thinking in the world, it's our secret weapon, it's why we are always one step ahead. So what is British Thinking? Well, it's combining things and creating something greater than those things, from those things. Sorry I can't be more specific.

British Thinking is using good old British Common Sense to find British solutions, to problems usually caused by other people. Now you know what British Thinking is, you will be able to solve my puzzle. By combining two or more components you will find the answers to life's problems.

In my big British larder I have seven ingredients, you need to work out the recipe to cook up…oh forget it this metaphor isn't working. Combine two or more of these things to create something greater than these things, from these things.

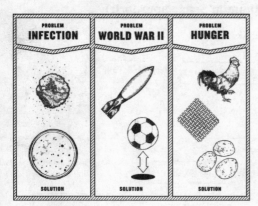

Answers overleaf

13

HAVE YOU GOT BRITISH THINKING? THE ANSWERS.

You knucklehead, you're looking at the answers, which means you can't work it out for yourself. Frankly, I'm not impressed.

However, you do need to grasp the simple British logic of British Thinking so I'm going to give you the answers. I can't have members of the British public walking around unarmed.

Infection: A Piece of Mould + Bloody Plate = Penicillin

World War II: Bomb + Bounce = Bouncing bomb

Hunger: Chicken + Weaving + Potatoes = Chicken in a Basket with Chips

It's British Common Sense!

EVERYONE HAS ASTHMA
(Common Sense approach)

Fig. 8 Asthma Flowchart

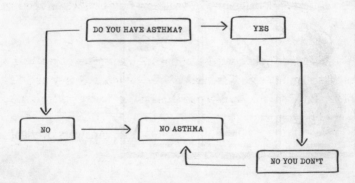

THE COMMON SENSE JUKEBOX

Common Sense tells us that there is now Too Much Music. No, hear me out. It's obvious to anyone with a pair of ears that they should just stop making new music, the stuff is piling up, there's no way you could ever get through it all in one lifetime and nor would you want to.

In my view music should have stopped some time around 1982[6] before Duran Duran had the chance to form. They are surplus to requirements: first out of the basket when the balloon starts going flat. In fact who let them into the balloon in the first place? Thinking about it, that's not a bad idea, someone send Duran Duran up in a faulty balloon now.

Anyway, in my gaff, we've got a jukebox and there's six CDs on there (it has the capacity for 164 but I don't feel the need for any more):

The first three need no explanation. The Old Testament of Rock, the New Testament of Rock, and a Third Testament of Rock (made up of leftover bits from the other two). You can't beat Queen, in the end you go back to the original fountain of rock and drink deep, or something.

The Essential Sixties compilation doesn't actually have any Beatles on it, so I'm not sure 'Essential' is the right word. Ropey might be better. But it has *Mr Tambourine Man* on it and a couple by Lulu so it does the job.

---

[6] Excepting all Queen records released after this date.

The Wet Wet Wet is in case any Jocks come in, and the U2 is for any passing Paddies. That's what I say, anyway. I'm not that happy about it because the title of it is 𝕬𝖈𝖍𝖙𝖚𝖓𝖌[7] Baby, which is 𝕲𝖊𝖗𝖒𝖆𝖓 for Hands Up Englander... Baby. It was a free demonstration disc that came with the jukebox, and I've tried all sorts to get the thing out of there. I had a go with the pliers only the other day, and all I managed to do was damage the edge. The edge of the disc, I mean, not the bloke in the band.

These CDs are popular in my pub because they are the only ones that get played, and they are the only ones that get played because they are the only ones that are there. Which makes me think that Popular Music only becomes popular because it's there. But then who am I to go thinking up theories, I am but an humble publican.

WHY THE MAGNA CARTA STILL MATTERS

That's where it all comes from folks – The Magna Carta – signed at Runnymede by King John. King John, brother of Richard the Lion-Heart, who died young – his body rejected the transplant, poor bastard. You know Prince John in the Robin Hood stories?[8] This is the same fella, only later on, after he got the promotion.

Here's how it happened at least how my dad used to tell it.

[7] 𝕲𝖊𝖗𝖒𝖆𝖓 word.
[8] See *BRITISH FOLK TALES*.

16

You see, King John was obsessed with putting up taxes – this was a long time ago, during the last Labour government – and the Barron Knights[9] weren't having it: like I said, this was ages ago, they were still having hits. So they take King John to one side and said, 'You're taking liberties mate!'

'What do you mean, liberties?' quoth King John.

And they all sort of shrugged and said, 'Um...dunno...?' so they had to go away and actually figure out what liberties were, and then which ones he was taking, and once they'd thought it through a bit and written them down they all ganged up on King John and got him to sign The Magna Carta, as well as a couple of their gold records too. They were still having hits back then. Fact is, they did a bloody good job. The Magna Carta explains why we're like we are. And it reads something like this (roughly):

Magna Carta

Do not speak unless you are spoken to

Nobody likes a smart arse[10]

Please keep off the grass

Get your round in on your way now

Drink up now

Each man is entitled to a trial by his peers

Come on we've all had a good laugh now

Please do not ask for credit as refusal often offends

No taxation without fair representation

Now most of these seem reasonable enough to me. And if you stop and look at yourself, the chances are they pretty much sum up what it's like to be part of this beautiful country. After all, in France they don't have Number 3: Please Keep Off The Grass. Instead they have Liberté, Egalité and Fraternité (Liberty, Equality and Fraternity, French words) which allows French people to walk wherever they like. As a result French parks are dustbowls and they have to play bowls in gravel, unlike our beautiful smooth lawns, which must be a total waste of time as you can't get the balls to roll in gravel. Timewasters. Common Sense isn't it?

[9] I've had my fair share of those. It's been a year.
[10] See *WE DON'T NEED NO HEDUCATION*.

THE BRITISH CHARACTER TRAITS THAT WHAT WHICH HAVE MADE US GREAT

These are the things that set us apart from other nations of the world, and the reasons we have been Top Dog for so long.

'BRITISH FAIR PLAY'

Look at the Zulu Wars, as seen in the film Zulu with Michael Caine.[11]The principal weapons the Zulu tribesman had at his disposal were spears, running fast, hiding, and there being a lot of him. We, the British, had guns. Now on the face of it this wasn't particularly fair, and this stuck in our British craws. So we turned up in bright red jackets to make ourselves nice and easy to spot, level the playing field a bit, make a contest of it. That's British Fair Play.

'MUSTN'T GRUMBLE'

We don't grumble in this country. 'Mustn't grumble!' said the British working man as his lung collapsed as a result of fumes from the pig iron during the Industrial Revolution; 'Mustn't grumble!' said the Tommy Redcoat as he was faced with disease, dysentery, poverty, and furious locals waving spears; 'Mustn't grumble!' said Tommy as he raised his rifle yet again.

---

[11] See *THE ZULU DRINKING GAME*.

Your average Frenchman on arrival in such a place would shrug his shoulders, say 'Bah! Non! Pas de tout! Ou est la gare! On y va!' and leave tout suite.[12] That's why we got an Empire and they got the top of Africa and the wrong end of Vietnam. 'Mustn't grumble!'

'FOLLOW THROUGH'

If there's one thing we've got in this country it's Follow Through. We see things through to their logical. Other nations lack this sense of Follow Through. The Italians for instance, folded early '43, then us and the 𝔊𝔢𝔯𝔪𝔞𝔫𝔰 smashed the place up for two years -- wonderful stuff, happy days. I've not checked, but did you know there's no Italian word for Follow Through? The 𝔊𝔢𝔯𝔪𝔞𝔫𝔰 don't have any Follow Through either, they got halfway to invading the UK and thought, you know what, it ain't worth it.

'REVOLUTION? NO THANKS'

We have never had one of those revolutions which resulted in lots of dead British people. We're too sensible for any of that nonsense. The only real revolution we had was the Pleasant Revolt way back in 13 something, and the Glorious Revolution in 1688 which was all about restoring the aristocracy to its rightful place. The one proper revolution we have had was the Industrial Revolution, during which we invented work. It was a classic no nonsense British revolution – Industrial Revolution, invented Industry. The clue is in the name.

---

[12] French words.

The French had a French Revolution, in which they invented being French, and in the process lots of French people were killed. 'Progress', say the historians and who am I to disagree. As far as I'm concerned the French are still disgusting, I mean revolting – bollocks got that one wrong. See what happens when you try to force things??

The Russians had a similar thing, but then there's an almost inexhaustible supply of Russians, so they could have a Revolution every other week if they liked. The last Revolution they had there got them a McDonalds in Red Square so maybe they won't be too keen on having another.

The Americans had a Revolution to get rid of us, and see how well that turned out for them, still fighting on the same side as us and speaking English. They really cut the old umbilical there didn't they, eh? (See *AMERICA, AMERICANS*).

'DISTINGUISHED OLD AGE'

America is a young country, like a teenager in many ways – doesn't know its own strength, doesn't listen, throws its weight around, noisy, obsessed with sex – whereas Great Britain is like a middle aged lady going through the menopause – forgetful, the occasional hot flush, loss of her manufacturing base, and constant fear of being usurped by a younger, prettier rival.

'THE GREAT BRITISH SENSE OF HUMOUR'

We have the greatest sense of humour in the world. There is no denying that. Benny Hill is world famous, all over the world. And the fact that only the simple and the slow like Benny Hill…? I rest my case.

'NEVER SAY DIE'

The British never say die. Unlike the **Germans** who say it all the time, as in the phrase: **'Die Englischer Pig Dog!'** And it's in those crucial two seconds, as he effortfully wraps his Teutonic tongue triumphantly around these tricky syllables, that Tommy Atkins pops him between the eyes and wins. Again. They started it.

'EVERYONE THINKS IN ENGLISH'

Now it is a crucial advantage that we the British have which is that everyone thinks in English. Indeed English is the natural language of the human being, it forms naturally in the human brain, as well as the brain of some animals like parrots, and the dog on *That's Life* who said 'sausages'. Everyone thinks in English, which is why when you go abroad (if you must) if you shout loudly enough IN ENGLISH their brain will reverberate in its original frequency and they will understand your precise meaning. They'll realise, 'Chips, Beer! I know what these things are', and go and get them. Waving your fists and your money helps too.

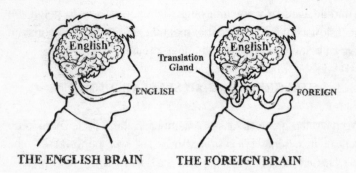

THE ENGLISH BRAIN   **THE FOREIGN BRAIN**

This is why we're permanently one step ahead of the **French**, they have to translate from the English in the brain to the French in their gob. This explains why French people are always going 'bah err umm err' because they can't remember the word for 'station' or 'croissant' or whatever. If a French bloke stubs his toe as he strolls up the boulevard, what happens is this – he thinks 'Bloody Hell, I've stubbed my toe!' then a split second later out comes the French translation: 'Zut alors! J'ai blessé mon pied!'[13]

This is why **Germans** seem stoic and tougher than us because **German** is an absolute nightmare to learn. It's not that they actually are tougher. I mean, you've got to know what you're going to say at the end of the sentence before you even start the beginning! You wouldn't be able to get up in the morning with that lot rattling around in your head. No wonder they have a cold breakfast. So, when a **German** stubs his toe he thinks 'Bloody Hell I've stubbed my bloody toe!' then he gets to work on translating what's in his head, 'Right Bloody Hell – um, I'll go for **'Donner und Blitzen, achtung Spitfeuer'** – no longer appropriate, I've – ah yes – **'ich habe'**, it's always 'ich habe' thank God for that, now stubbed – God, no idea – I'll make one up, **'gestübt'**, yeah that'll do, and that

13 French words.

23

goes at the end, result! **'Donner und Blitzen ich habe'** – my foot – ok, foot is **'fu'**, but is it masculine, feminine or neuter, arse, there's three. Well masculine that's blokes, feminine that's women and ships, neuter that's just things, a foot is a thing, so neuter of **'mein'** is **'meines'**, so that's it, **'Donner und Blitzen Ich Habe Meines Fub gestübt!'** Excellent, run it through one more time, **'Donner und Blitzen Ich Habe Meines Fub gestübt!'** Great!'

But by the time he's worked out what to say, by the time he has got his head around his Teutonic tongue, what's happened? The pain has left his foot, the moment's passed, *there's really no point in him saying anything at all!* And that's why the **Germans** appear to be tougher than us.

'THE BLITZ SPIRIT'

The **Germans** tried to break our spirit during the War by means of the Blitz, but the British People, being British, turned the tables and crushed their morale by gathering in underground stations and staging sing-a-long sing-song sing songs and raising our knees with knees ups. This was the Blitz Spirit, that showed that whatever was slung at us, the British People would find a way to keep going and hit back.

The Blitz Spirit can still be seen today. Look at those fat British mums passing chips and burgers through the school fences to their kids so they don't have to eat vegetables for school dinners. Back off Oliver![14] We know how to stick together during times of crisis. We saw off the V2 and the Doodlebug, we'll see off you and your goujons of celery, you fat-tongued Herbert.

[14] Yes, I am comparing Jamie Oliver to Hitler.

'NEVER FORGIVE, NEVER FORGET'

Even though we won World War Two, it has to be said we haven't forgotten, and we haven't forgiven. And this rings true across the board – has anyone really forgiven Spain for the Armada, even though we defeated them back then in 1588, it's still fresh; the French may have fought on our side in the last two world wars but who can forget – or forgive – Napoleon?

And as for the Vikings, why my blood boils at the very thought. And the other thing we never do, MR BLAIR, is never apologise.[15] Nice one Tony. This may look like grudge bearing but in fact all it is is a question of remaining alert at all times, and knowing your history. Thank God someone's on their toes.

'POPULARITY'

Above all we're really popular and everyone likes us. What's not to like?

[15] I know he's retired, but it's not like it's anyone else's fault. I hope he tries running a pub now he's retired and he can see exactly what a nightmare 24 hour opening actually is.

HOW TO SURVIVE A CAR CONVERSATION DOWN THE PUB

I have to say it fills me with dismay when punters start talking to me about matters automotical in the pub. Don't get me wrong, I like sitting on the toilet reading *AutoTrader* for half an hour as much as the next man, (although I prefer it if there's no-one sat next to me).

Truth be told, though, I feel the old shutters coming down any time the subject rears its four-wheeled-head in my gaff. The real problem is that it's a sure-fire way to scare women out of any conversation. So when the first girl to cross the threshold for something like six months comes over, Steve, she doesn't want to hear about the new alloys on your Punto, and nor do I you turnip.

The truth is I haven't even passed my test[16] and the car I bought for investment purposes is up on bricks in a lock-up. The trouble is I've forgotten where the lock-up is which is something of a drawback. From what I can remember though, from the ad in *AutoTrader*, it's a Daimler Sovereign, it's got about 258,000 miles give or take, it definitely needs a new engine and hasn't got any wheels (hence why the bloody thing is up on bricks, keep up). Also if my memory serves me correctly the passenger door doesn't lock. Mind you, they only wanted £695, so now who looks stupid? I also bought it because I thought it would be the perfect Shag Wagon but unfortunately it has only ever served to remind me, in grim metaphorical form, of my sex life, i.e. up on bricks. (An entire year.)

I used to have a Granada, which is now a hotbed of iron oxide at the bottom of the canal[17] round the back of the pub. And, let me tell you, what a night that was. I just wish I could remember how I got out as it sank to the bottom. Perhaps the fact that the driver's window was a gaffered-over Corn Flake box helped. See, talking about cars like that is alright, but, you know, talking about cars in the how-many-horsepower and nought-to-sixty sense frankly impresses no one.

When people talk to me about cars I normally deflect them by mentioning the time I met David Coulthard. (I have, did I mention that.) This normally puts them well off their stroke while I go down and pretend to change a barrel. Now there's a bloke, what a top man. People say he looks glum, but be fair. If you'd been

[16] After nine attempts you have the skills base anyway, and anyone can be unlucky on the day.
[17] See *WHAT TO DO WHEN YOUR CAR FALLS INTO A RIVER.*

sprayed in the face with French champagne by some **German** to the sound of the Italian national anthem every fortnight for the best part of a decade, you'd be gloomy. I know I would.

Now, obviously you won't be able to do this. You haven't met David Coulthard. I have, did I mention that. So when a car conversation starts up down your pub, you'll have to stand there nodding and agreeing, thinking of some way you can take someone else's comment and change the words around a bit to make it sound like a new point of view. I've seen it done a thousand times.

Don't panic, though, help is at hand. This is what this book is all about. Here are a few lines that will help you sound like you know what you're talking about. These are all generic and form a five-point plan suited to nearly any conversation to do with cars you're ever likely to find yourself in.

One last thing: Good luck, it's a jungle out there.

#1 QUESTIONS BEST LEFT UNASKED

'Is this mini cab insured?'

?

DO'S & DON'TS
of car conversation

CHECK SHEET

(Mr)/Mrs/Ms   Model: Mondeo   Make: Coupe

Year: 86   Colour: Puce   Odometre reading: 133785

DO	DON'T
☑ **DO** say, you drive an Aston Martin DB7. It impresses the ladies.	☒ **DON'T** say, you drive an Aston Martin DB7 if you actually don't; remember your Mondeo is parked just outside the window.
☑ **DO** use the proper jargon when talking about cars; there's nothing worse than ignorance.	☒ **DON'T** use the word coupé, not in my pub.
☑ **DO** say, you bought the Land Rover because if you get involved in a 'head on' you want to come out of it 'in one piece'/'top dog'/'alive'	☒ **DON'T** say, you bought the Land Rover because it's the only vehicle you really feel can cope with towing the yacht down to Chichester.
☑ **DO** say, you've just bought a brand new Jaguar S-Type diesel Saloon, six cylinder, all the trimmings bastard of a machine.	☒ **DON'T** say, you've just bought a brand new Jaguar S-Type diesel Saloon, six cylinder, all the trimmings bastard of a machine…if you're putting your car up in a late night poker game and you know full well the wife's Fiesta is in the drive.
☑ **DO** say, you can't remember how the hell you ended up in the canal, but it was a great night up until then.	☒ **DON'T** say, you, can't remember how the hell you ended up in the canal but it was a great night up until then…officer.

Serial number

PL0034095

MURRAY MOTORS
LONDON EC1 PL
020 7050 3780
REG: 2559

Follow these Common Sense guidelines and you'll be fine, don't panic.

WHY BRITISH INVENTORS SPEND ALL THEIR TIME COVERING THE ARSE OF THE REST OF THE WORLD

A few examples to back up the title. Well I wouldn't just write a title and not have anything to say now would I?

1) The French are the masters of wine and produce over twenty percent of the wine in the world and have supposedly been doing so since around 300 BC. Brilliant. Well done. *Vive la France.* But what were you doing until 1795? I'll tell you, you were sitting on your French behinds surrounded by the finest wines waiting for the British Inventor Reverend Samuel Henshall to invent the **Corkscrew**: until he came along they couldn't get the bastards open. Timewasters. If it wasn't for us, you'd still be drinking that cheap wine that comes in boxes.[18] This wouldn't be the last time we helped the French out in a time of crisis.

2) Cornelius Jacobszoon Drebbel, a Dutchman, started work on the submarine at the beginning of the seventeenth Century: funny that, because it wasn't until 1902 that Brit Simon Lake invented the **Periscope**. Just how did that clog-wearing buffoon figure he was going to navigate? Must have been stoned. As usual.

[18] It also puts into question what Jesus was drinking at the Last Supper. I can't imagine Luke trying to open the red with his Biro.

3) In 1903 a certain Mr P. W. Litchfield of the Goodyear Tyre Company patented the first tubeless tyre. That means for eighteen years prior the people of **Germany** had to listen to the screech of metal on macadam as Karl Benz was sliding around trying to think of a solution whilst attempting to negotiate corners in a tyreless motor vehicle. Timewaster. Inventing the car before the bloody wheels were ready: like wiping your backside before taking a dump.

4) The first postal system can be dated back to Iran possibly as early as the 6th Century BC, but until we invented **stamps** on the 1st May 1840 those letters were going nowhere! A backlog of 24 centuries of undelivered mail solved overnight, by us, the British.

5) In 1884 British man James Forbes invented the ***Seismometer*** which is amazing considering we don't have earthquakes.[19]

IN CONCLUSION

The British are not too self-conscious to help the world out. We'll put our hand up and say we've got an idea, however simple. They also say the British suffer from the stiff upper lip, that we don't talk about embarrassing topics and that we're uncomfortable with natural bodily functions. Well if that's so then how come it was us that invented not only the Flushing Toilet but Toilet Paper? No, we don't mind dealing with shit, after all we've been putting up with the rest of the world since we can remember.

[19] We don't have earthquakes as God is British, and you don't shit on your own doorstep do you?

WHAT WOMEN WANT

Sigmund Freud asked the question, 'What is it that women want?' and failed of course to find the answer. But it's obvious, isn't it? They want the central heating turned up, don't they?

TOP TEN MOVIES

Common Sense tells us that there are now Too Many Films. No, hear me out. It's obvious to anyone with a pair of eyes that they should just stop making new films, they're piling in huge piles of DVD releases and box sets and musty videos, that there will never be time to watch 'em all in one lifespan.

Films should have stopped some time around 1982, before Duran Duran had the chance to do a Bond theme. I actually think the last film they should have made is *Where Eagles Dare*, but we'll get to that. After *Where Eagles Dare* cinema had pretty much said all it would ever say.

Anyway, what we have here is essential viewing top ten pub conversation movies. They also happen to be my favourite top ten movies of all time (apart from one of them, but it remains essential viewing for that reason). You will note that none of these are French films, only one of them is black and white, none of them involve crying at any point, none of them are on the usual film critics' lists of films that changed the world because after all there's no way a film is going to change the world is there, though that *Panorama* with Diana[20] in it made a few waves.

10) **The Italian Job:** the classic caper movie, they just don't make them like this any more, as the shabbily woeful remake proved, though it does go on a bit, especially once they've blown the bloody doors off.

9) **Zulu:** Michael Caine looking steely in his redcoat, the brave tale of the men holding out at Rorke's Drift against unimaginable odds, and winning. Those Zulu chants translate pretty much directly as 'get off my land'. Farmers. Goes on a bit during Welsh parts.[21]

[20] She was a candle in the wind.
[21] See THE ZULU DRINKING GAME.

8) **The Dambusters:** if you like your upper lips stiff (and who doesn't?) this is the place to go. In this day and age he'd have got the week off cos his dog was run over and he'd have sued the RAF for post-traumaticbla bla bla. They Bust the Dams, the clue's in the name. Goes on a bit in the build-up to the raid itself.

7) **The Battle of Britain:** we won it the first time round no help from no one else, then we made a film and won it all over again no help from no one else. Goes on a bit at the end. I like seeing Heinkels[22] hurtling to their doom in flames as much as the next Brit, but we know the result, we could all have been in the pub half an hour earlier if the Luftwaffe had just thrown in the towel once it was obvious they weren't going to beat The Few.

6) **Escape to Victory:** utterly far-fetched this one. Football. Prisoner of war camp. Stallone with blood on his face. Yanks playing football and winning. Like I said, utterly far-fetched. You have to see this film, as it will make you enjoy all other films – no matter how bad any film you may be watching is, it isn't Escape to Victory. And it goes on a bit.

It's rubbish. No argument.

---

[22] Though in the film the planes look like Heinkels He111s they are in fact Spanish planes, Construcciones Aeronáuticas SA 2.111s. These looked pretty much the same though they were ironically powered by the beautiful British Rolls Royce Merlin engine, like off a Spitfire (see *THE SUPERMARINE SPITFIRE MKS 1-26*). You learn something new every day, don't you?

5) **A Bridge Too Far:** in which Sean Connery fails to capture the bridge, Anthony Hopkins does capture the bridge but then loses it, Michael Caine arrives late at the bridge, Robert Redford paddles a boat under the bridge, and the Germans talk about the bridge in real German with real subtitles. What else could you possibly want? Goes on a bit.

Ah, Mister Bond, I've been expecting you...

4) **Ice Cold in Alex:** the nerve-shredding tale of desert warfare, mind games, treachery, an ambulance and a beer at the end. The way he necks that pint has to be one of cinema's greatest moments. Goes on a bit though, especially in the middle.

3) **The Eagle Has Landed:** actually I can't remember this one, I think I've got it confused with *Where Eagles Dare...*

2) **Walkabout:** Jenny Agutter. Buff. Doesn't go on anything like long enough.

1) **Where Eagles Dare.**

WHERE EAGLES DARE

Where Eagles Dare is a film unlike any other you have seen, unless you've seen *The Wild Geese, The Guns of Navarone, Kelly's Heroes, The Eagle Has Landed, Wild Geese 2* or *The Dirty Dozen.*

Basically, the whole thing is about a crack team of British commandos, and Clint Eastwood, who are sent to rescue an American general from a castle in 𝕲𝖊𝖗𝖒𝖆𝖓𝖞 by the man who was the voice of Paddington Bear. Forgive me if you've seen the film, but unbelievably there's a whole lot of people out there under 26 who don't even know about WW2 so you can't expect them to know about this classic movie.

What you notice nowadays about *Where Eagles Dare* is how slow it is. Clint doesn't speak for an entire twenty minutes, he just sits around looking moody. Richard Burton – bless him for all he did for the trade – is Britain's top agent despite being a middle-aged man who is obviously somewhat out of shape (seeing him scramble through the snow ain't pretty). This is one of those films where 𝕲𝖊𝖗𝖒𝖆𝖓𝖘 speak in suspicious 𝕲𝖊𝖗𝖒𝖆𝖓 accents, but when Burton and Clint are talking to 𝕲𝖊𝖗𝖒𝖆𝖓𝖘 in (presumably) 𝕲𝖊𝖗𝖒𝖆𝖓 they

Pointless random love interest
for when there's no fighting.

carry on talking in their own accents, and don't bother pretending that they're talking **German** by doing a **German** accent. In fact there's a whole scene where the two of them sit in a bar with horrendous **German** folk music (further proof the Nazis were evil) and talk about what's going on and you can't tell whether they are supposed to be speaking **German** or English or what. This isn't the only inconsistency in the movie – at one point **Germans** are seen to be laughing, which as we all know doesn't happen.[23]

Once in the castle the world's most tedious double cross scene is acted out whilst the creepy SS officer with funny lips who looks like a Nazi Party Pearly King is trying to chat up the blonde woman Clint and Burton have brought with them for no good reason, apart from it's someone for Burton to snog with in that strange 1960s waggly-headed way. The double cross scene includes a Fräulein (who is a qualified nurse) with a giant ludicrous hairdo, the kind of hairdo that if you were trapped in the middle of a global war you simply wouldn't have time to do, because there was a war on and there are more important things to worry about than a three hour hairdo. After this scene things really kick off and Clint gets stuck into an endless supply of **Germans**, none of whom can shoot straight.

Then you get the world's nastiest cable car fight, with Burton huffing and puffing his way through two middle-aged traitors in giant parkas. This culminates with the Welsh wizard sticking an ice axe in one geezer's forearm, and then jumping from one cable car to another as they pass in opposite directions high above the valley. These days, of course, tiny Tom Cruise might do such a thing and you wouldn't even blink. Back then, though,

[23] Did you know there is no **German** word for funny?

film stars were built differently, and every time I watch this I'm convinced that this time Burton is going to take the second cable car plummeting down with him.

Fighting on top of cable cars is a direct contravention of EU Health and Safety law. Another reason I'm against Europe.

What's really amazing about *Where Eagles Dare* is that World War Two is jam packed with incredible true stories of genuine derring-do, fantastic tales of self-sacrifice and endurance, but when it came to making a World War Two adventure movie they thought, 'You know what? Let's just make it up'. Though this isn't to say that this classic war movie isn't top notch in every way.

Goes on a bit, though. Anyhow, in my gaff we've devised the perfect way to help this movie slip along for when it comes on your screens again (May Bank Holiday? Boxing Day? Don't panic it'll be on either or both. And again when the Snooker World Final finishes unexpectedly early...)[24]

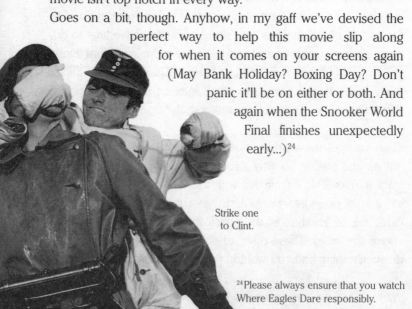

Strike one to Clint.

[24] Please always ensure that you watch Where Eagles Dare responsibly.

THE DRINKING GAME

Basically the rules are simple: keep an eye on the movie and whenever something from our list occurs, take a drink. Here goes, see you on the other side:

† Every time you hear 'damned', **take a drink.**

† Whenever anyone says 'agent', **take a drink.**

† **Take a drink** every time it is clear that our heroes are 'not there' and a back projection is being used.

† 'Gentlemen, see you after the war!', **drain your glass.**

† First time the castle appears go and **get another drink;** also a good time to have a piss, make any outstanding phone calls, do VAT...

† **Take a drink** when Clint finally speaks.

† Every time a Nazi clicks his heels **take a drink.**

† Every time it's obviously a double doing the stunt, get someone else to **have a drink** for you.

† Every time a German is killed **take a drink,** though bear in mind Clint takes out something in the region of eighty to eighty five Germans in this movie, so you're looking at a proper skinful.

† If a car blows up for no good reason other than it's going downhill, **take a drink.**

† This should be more than enough to get completely slaughtered, but if you want to have a really hard core session, add this to the mix: Every 'Broadsword calling Danny Boy', **take a drink.**

GOOD LUCK TOMMY!!

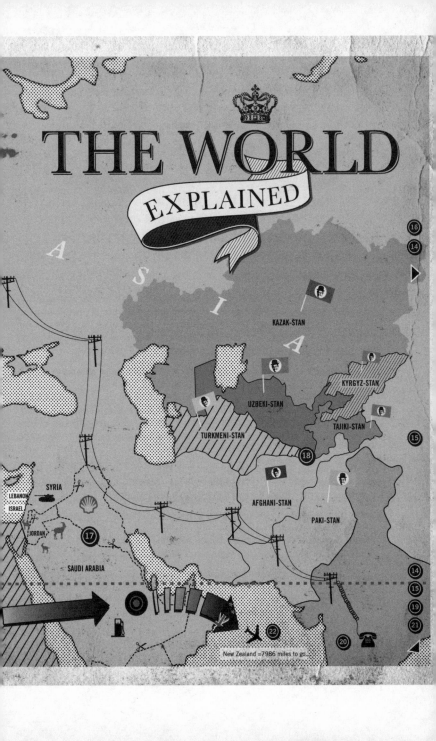

THE WORLD
EXPLAINED

A S I A

KAZAK-STAN

UZBEKI-STAN

KYRGYZ-STAN

TURKMENI-STAN

TAJIKI-STAN

AFGHANI-STAN

PAKI-STAN

SYRIA

LEBANON
ISRAEL
JORDAN

SAUDI ARABIA

New Zealand =7986 miles to go.

At the top in the middle, not round the arse end like Australia. Great Britain is the Centre Of The Earth.

It's a scientific fact, straight through the middle runs the nought line of longitude. Alright, we put the line there but it still stands – Great Britain is the Centre Of The Earth. And this means that we the British are in charge of what time it is all over the world. The Germans don't sit down for their lunch until we say it's one o'clock. And because they're an hour out they're not even eating their lunch at lunchtime. Ha ha, that's showed them.

The world runs to Greenwich Meantime, GMT, not Paris Meantime, PMT. Imagine the chaos. You'd get nothing done. Well, no, you'd get everything done, exactly as you were asked, and come back bearing chocolates. Oh yeah, we wrote the book and it's in English. The finest language in the world. A language spoken all over the planet and even in space as any fan of Star Trek will tell you. A language so easy to speak even Americans can handle it with some degree of skill.

Great Britain is the most beautiful country in the world without a doubt, you'd cheat on your wife with Great Britain if she offered, though she wouldn't because she's not that sort of country.

Being at the top in the middle of the map means the whole of the world looks up to us. And now thanks to tourism the whole of the world looks us up too. The thing to remember when you look at the rest of the world is that secretly deep down all of the other countries wish they were Great Britain, they're all jealous basically.

And of course it's worth remembering that Great Britain is current World War Champion Of The World: undisputed, thousand year clean sheet at all weights, though now we're fighting lighter than we used to, strictly speaking the Yanks work for us, which keeps us at heavyweight.

② Ireland

Next door there's our cheeky sidekick Ireland: motorbike and sidecar, they'd be going nowhere without us, oh they've painted it a different colour but we're the ones with the engine. Now I'm the first to admit it's been a bumpy ride with the Irish, things haven't always gone according to plan. And although I'm not one for those big apologies about historical events, I am prepared to say sorry for the Potato Famine, shocking, terrible event. Mind you, you couldn't get crisps for love nor money in London at the time. That's when we first turned to the peanut in the trade, you gotta keep the punters thirsty somehow.

③ France

The Neighbour From Hell: France. Or 'The France' as they prefer to call it, La France[25], The France in case we should confuse it with some other France, This France or That France or Reliable Courageous Turning Up In Times Of Battle France.

I don't know why we don't just grow a great big hedge up the English Channel and spoil their light. That or a big noisy party in Kent, lob some dog dirt over the fence. The French have lost the plot completely: they've got a town called Brest and none of them think it's funny. Pathetic, childish.

④ Spain and Portugal

Next to that you've got the unsolved Rubik's cube that is Spain and Portugal.[26] Truth be told we've got a whole book to fill, but even then Portugal's not going to make the cut. Spain is a strange place where they think nothing of fighting animals. Absurd: I'd never punch a cow, that would be humiliating for it on the way to its death. I have no row with a cow, I want no battle with cattle. I might lamp a squirrel, but that would be purely because of the ongoing turf war about the sandpit next to the swing in the beer garden. If I was to punch a squirrel I certainly wouldn't do it dressed up in tights and a dodgy hat and prance around making a big song and dance of it, I certainly wouldn't stick pins in the squirrel first to enrage it, I wouldn't wave a cape the colour squirrels hate to get it annoyed, which is probably grey-green like a rotten nut, I don't know, I wouldn't do it.

[25] French words.
[26] They couldn't get those last two bricks.

Anyway, for years the Spaniards were convinced the world was flat, I mean come on! It's not even level. Bloody 'ell Carlos look around you, the mountains are a clue. And what's worse they had to be proved wrong by an Italian ... that must have hurt, in fact it hurt so bad that when they got to America they set about killing everyone they could get their hands on just because they were embarrassed.

⑤ Italy

Italy is called the Boot of Europe of course, but only by people with nothing better to say. In general there is a problem with Italians and their inability to follow things through. Look at the place: the Coliseum, still hasn't got a roof on it; Venice, they still haven't called a plumber, there's a stop cock under the stairs surely; Pompeii – tidy up! And what is a pizza? It's a pasty that some lazy bastard hasn't shut yet. Shut the pasty Giuseppe!!

⑥ Switzerland

Then you've got Switzerland: and you have to stop, pause and wonder at how they must cope. Look at the situation they've got themselves into – French to the right of 'em, Austrians to the left of 'em, Germans up above, Italians down below. You'd never sell that flat would you? No matter how tidy it was or how many chocolates you left lying around.

⑦ Sweden

Bloody Swedes, next time they ask for our help we'll leave out the Allen key.

⑧ Denmark

After the diesel ban in 1953 they had to rely on fat men with beards to pull their lorries.

⑨ Austria

It's made of pastry and that's why it's shrunk.

⑩ Eastern Europe

Romania, Moldavia, Bulgaria, the Womble countries.

Poland

(11)

The best tradesmen in the world, fact. Which is why we changed the rules so they could come and work over here. And now it's empty the Germans are no longer interested.

Germany

(12)

They've been too quiet for too long. Mind you, you have to respect the Germans, two cracks at the world title.

Yugoslavia

(13)

Yugoslavia – now basically the problem in Yugoslavia is that the people who live there don't really get on. It's very complicated and at the same time not complicated at all. So a while back we bombed the place to make it simpler. Well, you can't argue about who lives where when there are no houses left. The lesson we learned there though is that there's no pleasing some people.

International Date Line

(14)

International Date Line – which we the British set up a while back so that middle-aged men from Birmingham could meet and marry ladies from the Philippines.

China

(15)

Recently the Chinese have successfully put a man into space. They didn't use a rocket for this, no, they just stood on each other's shoulders and passed him up. Hence the leotard shortage of a few years ago. China is of course the country you could never go to war with, it's Common Sense. There's not enough bullets. And if you wanted to get enough bullets you'd have to get them made in China. And then they might smell a rat: 'More bullets please Mr Ping?…Oh I don't know, about 4 billion… None of your business mate!'

Mongolia

(16)

Mongolia – of course, can't call it that any more, bloody social workers. Same goes for the Black Sea. Can't say anything these days can you?

The Middle East

The Middle East – very complicated place the Middle East. In fact it's so complicated that me trying to explain it here on the page could possibly make it worse. But it's worth a try and this is a book of Common Sense, which they could do with a healthy dose of. Basically the people who live there don't really get on. They should pull their heads in the lot of 'em. Put the kettle on before you do anything hasty, count to ten, I don't know. Basically it's a four thousand year dispute about whose goats go where. The Israelis: I don't like the people at the end of my road, but I haven't bought a tank. Of course the problem with buying a tank is once you've bought one, then you've got to use it.

We stepped in a while back to help sort out the Middle East once and for all, sat down with a red pen and a ruler and drew them some nice straight borders around the naturally occurring oil that we had found that they weren't looking for. Camels don't run on derv do they? And then we sorted them out with Kings and Queens and uniforms and countries with nice Arab names like Syria and Jordan and Saudi Arabia when we could have just called them Shell, Esso, BP, Texaco, Wild Bean Café. You'd think they'd be more grateful.

The Stans

Look here in the middle bit of the world and you have all the 'Stans. Kazakhstan where the Kazaks are from, Uzbekistan where Uzbekis are from, Olliandstan where Stan and Ollie are from, and Kzrgyztzzzstan where the Kzrgyztzzzs are from. And then there's Pakistan where Asians are from.

Christmas Island

Christmas Island – where it is Christmas every day – send Wizzard there and they can knock it off.

India

Or 118-dia as I call it. Apparently the Geordies asked for too much money. I have to say that people are pretty much unreasonable about the phone service they receive from Indian call centres. Imagine the scene, it's four in the morning and your slumber is rudely broken by the phone ringing and some nerk from Loughborough demanding the number for Pizza Hut. What would you do? You'd mutter the first eight digits that came into your head, slam the phone down and go back to bed.

(21) Australia

Now I love Ozzies, beautiful people, genetically engineered for bar work. New South Wales – as if we needed one. Still if you're going to have one have it as far away as possible, and as inhospitable to the Welsh as possible: no valleys, no coal, no English people to complain about. As for Queensland – it's all the Queen's land thank you very much.

(22) New Zealand

28 hours of connecting flights to wind up in Scotland. No thanks.

(23) Antarctica

We of course were second to get to the South Pole. I'm happy to admit that. Because we were second to get there we able to verify that the other bloke got there first which meant that strictly speaking we're the umpire on that one therefore: our game, our rules, we win.

(24) Hawaii

The place with a Page Three girl's name and home to Pearl Harbour where the Americans were taken completely and utterly by surprise … two years into a Global War. I ask you. Amateurs.

(25) Galapagos Islands

Where Charles Darwin (British) invented evolution.

(26) Tropic Of Cancer

They should change that one, it's tasteless and upsetting for the relatives.

(27) The Falkland Islands

1982, no help from no one else. Oh yeah: wet, windy and nowhere near here – definitely ours. And that wasn't a war for oil, the kind the Guardian don't like, no that was a war for penguins which as everyone knows are an essential ingredient in stout, you boil 'em up and the white stuff floats to the top.

(28) Peru

I have never been to Peru and I'm not going to go. I'm no bleeding heart but this is my personal protest against the way they treat their bear population. It's an outrage, the way every bear is taken to one side, given a hat and a coat, a suitcase and a covering note, a one way ticket to the UK, taken to the ship and told to piss off out of Peru. It's disgusting: coming over here eating our marmalade sandwiches.

(29) Colombia

Where excitement's from.

(30) Venezuela

Capital city Caracas – grow up. You can't have a city that rhymes with maracas.

(31) Panama

One canal – I for one am unimpressed. Not only did we the British invent the canal, we've got thousands and they all lead to Great Britain not the arse end of nowhere like theirs.

(32) Mexico

Capital city Mexico City. Make an effort.

(33) America

Basically, the best way of summing up America is that it's a good idea that's got out of hand. Timewasters – it's not San Andreas' fault is it? It's theirs for building the town there in the first place. Typical American tactic, blaming some poor bloody Mexican. Rocky Mountains – well of course they are.
See *AMERICA, AMERICANS.*

(34) Canada

Canada looks big on the map, but only the first three miles above America are at all habitable without having to wear tennis rackets for shoes or whatever you have to do in countries where it snows a lot, and you can't just use the fall of 3 inches of snow as an excuse to not go into work because of gridlock or whatever.

But the most interesting thing about Canada is that there's a whole bunch of people who live there who are absolutely convinced that they're French. I know, unbelievable. But they're not French, they're just living somewhere shit and it's a reflex action. They're only human.

(35) Baffin Island

Not a baffin on it.

(36) Greenland

Which is white.

(37) Iceland

Which is a Volcano.

(38) Pharaoh Islands

Which is nowhere near Egypt.

> When God, who is British, made the World, He made it round and he made it this way for a reason. It's so if you are unfortunate to have to pass through one of these terrible places, no matter which one, if you keep on going you will always end up back in Her Majesty's Great Britain. And that is why the world is round and how we know God is British.

GRADUATE TRAINEES
(Spare Me)

My personal nightmare (apart from the one with Bill Oddie in a nightdress holding a lamp pointing at my naked form and screaming: 'Look at those badgers coming out of their set!') is the thought of my pub being handed over to some graduate trainee. And what is a graduate trainee? Someone with a piece of paper that says he's qualified to tell me what to do even though *he's never pulled a pint in his life!*

Now, as I understand it, this is not a trend that confines itself to my trade. In offices up and down this proud nation, men and women who are perfectly good at their jobs are being told what to do by some kid who's just got out of a college, where they've done little more than eat crisps and watch telly in an ironic manner for three years, and who's on four times the money yet they know eff all about eff all. I for one will not be told what to do by someone who was born *after* the Falklands War, so why should you?

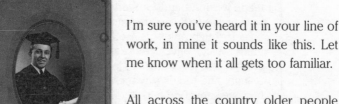

HE'S NEVER PULLED A PINT IN HIS LIFE

I'm sure you've heard it in your line of work, in mine it sounds like this. Let me know when it all gets too familiar.

All across the country older people who know the job perfectly well are being bundled aside to make way for these muppets, and now it's time to fight back.

50

the GRADUATE TRAINEE

1) He's 22, he's never pulled a pint in his life

2) He keeps making hilarious (and I use the word sarcastically) references to Deal or No Deal[27], which after all, he sat on a sofa for the last two years peering at through a marijuana haze.

3) Doesn't know one end of a peanut from the other, let alone the dry roast from the salted

4) Goes on about the pub and its potential as a retail outlet, not a boozer, not a gaff, not a local

5) Asks me to come up with something called a 'mission statement'. A mission statement! Do I look like Tom Cruise? Toe-rag

6) Uses the word 'Clientele' – French word of course

7) He's a Graduate Trainee, yes, but I have every suspicion that until the year before last that place was at Carpentry College

8) Comes in with his graphs and flow charts and demographics and customer indexes and booze per square inch ratios and thinking outside the box marketing notions and he's never pulled a pint in his life!!

9) Keeps going on about his plans for an out of town super-pub on the ring road. It's a warehouse basically with Tex-Mex in. Says it's the future. Says it all, basically

10) He's never pulled a pint in his life

The trouble is although I run the pub for the brewery I am in many ways my own boss, whilst not actually being my own boss. So to have this infant toe-rag come in and tell me the hows and whys of my trade which I was raised into man and boy is beyond the pale. So, and I'm not proud to relate this but I might as well and you are welcome to use it if you want, I took advantage of his youth and inexperience and got shot of him. Basically his behaviour forced me into taking the embarrassing though necessary action of telling the regulars that he is in fact a bed-wetter in order to get rid of him. He didn't last long after that. Like I said, I'm not proud of myself for having done that, but it worked.

[27] Which is a guessing game, let's not fool ourselves about this. Those poor people with their systems. Let's Guess What's In The Box just doesn't have the same ring. Nice to see Noel back though, innit? They'll never replace the old stars will they?

GREAT BRITISH SPORTING INSTITUTIONS

Britain is the Top Sporting Nation. Of course it is. It's Common Sense. The British character is innately sporting, sportsmanship flows through our British veins, and we believe in the fundamental values of fair play for the simple reason that we invented it.[28]

No other nation on the planet has invented more sports than us, and what's more all ours work perfectly. We even put in some deliberately grey areas, such as offside and LBW, just to make sure we'd have something to argue about. That's how good we are at inventing sports.

Look at the sports the Yanks have come up with. Baseball? Well, they just nicked rounders, didn't they, off some British girls school, and added extra spitting.

American Football? Just rugby with advert breaks. They didn't even have the imagination to think of a special new name for it, just nicked our word football and stuck their word American in front of it. American football is a pantomime and they're all dressed up as dames. Still, in fairness, if you actually like to crouch down with your backside in the air shouting out incomprehensible sequences of numbers then maybe it's for you. Basketball? A great spectacle if your idea of entertainment is two teams of improbably freakish giants taking it in turns to score.

[28] Did you know that the **German** word for 'fair play' is the same as the word for 'weakness'?

And what about our European neighbours? The French have given us *boules*, which in many ways is similar to the British game of bowls, except that the French have removed from the equation the necessity to grow and tend to a lawn, which is too much like hard work for them.[29] The Spanish, when they weren't enjoying a range of sports designed around the destruction of livestock, put their heads together and gave the world *pelota*, where two blokes throw a ball at a wall using shopping baskets, which is not so much a sport, more a way of passing the time while you wait for the queue at the *supermercado* tills to go down. The **Germans** invented leather shorts and torture, and never really moved on to sports.

No, we are the top sporting nation, which is why our great sporting institutions are the envy of the world.

WIMBLEDON

The Best Tennis Tournament In The World. It's the one they all want to win. All right, so there are supposedly four major tournaments, your Wimbledon, the American Open, the Aussie open, and the French Open, but ask any French, Aussie or American tennis player which tournament he wants to win the most and he'll tell you: 'Wimbledon'. This is because it's the best. There's a chance you might spot Her Majesty, and we use grass to play on, which is how tennis is meant to be. Lawn Tennis, that's its full title, and the clue's in the name. It's not called Red Muck Tennis is it? But you try telling that to the blokes down at Roland Garros. And even though it's donkey's years since a Brit actually won Wimbledon – it's our own fault, we made all the

[29] See *WHY THE MAGNA CARTA STILL MATTERS.*

others *want* it too much – we're not all that bothered, because with strawberries at a fiver each we're making all that prize money back on the catering.

THE BRITISH GRAND PRIX

The Best Motor Racing Race In The World. Whether at Silverstone, at Brands Hatch, or at ancient Brooklands, the British know how to do a Grand Prix. We don't always win, but it's our podium whether we're on it or not. The only mystery to me is how we managed to let them get away with giving the whole sport a French name for so long. See, we, the British, send the cars around a specially-built racing track that we've put in the time and trouble to provide, that way we find out which car and which driver is the fastest. In France, when it's their turn, they use the streets of Monaco, already the pokiest little city on the continent and not even in France, and just close it to normal traffic for a couple of hours. Unbelievable. They go to no trouble at all. You'd almost have to salute their ability to do the Bare Minimum[30] if it wasn't for the fact that they are French and so are quite simply slacking off. And it's all designed to make it easier for the French drivers, isn't it, who surge into a healthy lead while all the others are trying to make head or tail of fold-up tourist maps.

[30] See *BARE MINIMUM, DOING, THE.*

WEMBLEY

The Best Stadium In The World. It was already the best football stadium in the world before they pulled it all down, sold off the pitch in half-a-metre-square bits, and built a new stadium in the same place, so imagine what it's like now that it's £757 million better. It's got to be fantastic, hasn't it, like the stadium of the future, on the moon or something, with hover seats and telly helmets for everyone. It has always been every footballer's dream to step out onto the hallowed turf... I hope the new stadium made sure to get hallowed turf. I wonder if they had to get it specially hallowed? Do they grow it at a vicarage and only water it with water from the font that's been used for baptising babies? Or did they have a hallowing machine left over from when they pulled down the old

The greatest sporting moment in all human history that I remember clearly even though it happened two years before I was born.

place...? Anyway, it's every footballer's dream to play at Wembley, whatever country he comes from, because it's the best, and sometimes this does cause a problem. Sometimes foreign players can get so excited about playing at Wembley, the home of football, that they play way above their natural level of performance, which makes it that much more difficult for England to beat them. Someone somewhere didn't Think That One Through.

THE BOAT RACE

The Best Rowing Race In The World. Some miserable types like to have a go at the old Boat Race, don't they? Why is it always Oxford versus Cambridge? Why don't they let some other teams join in? Why don't they have semi-finals? The fact is that the best rowers in the world all end up at Oxford or Cambridge sooner or later, it's just Common Sense. If they want to take part in the best rowing race in the world, then obviously they're going to go to one of the two universities that takes part in it. That's why the Boat Race teams always seem to consist of one token really posh bloke to do the interviews, a tiny woman who weighs less than half an oar, and seven six-foot-nine-inch Canadians who are taking spurious degrees in subjects like Pointy Boat Mechanics or Water Displacement Theory.

THE LORD'S TEST MATCH

The Best Cricket Match In The World. At The Best Cricket Ground In The World. All the international touring teams get to play a test match at Lord's. It's their dream, because it's the best, and the Home of Cricket. It's inspiring, the Grace Gates, the Nursery End, that walk from the changing room, through the Long Room, past all the portraits of the greats, past the honours boards with all the names of the great batsmen who've scored centuries down the years, and the great bowlers who've taken five-for...Too bloody inspiring, actually. That's why all the visiting players play out of their skins and we never win there. Only one cricket ground comes close to Lord's anywhere in the world, and that's The Oval, which is ours as well, though it being so special causes similar problems *vis a vis*[31] the other teams winning.

THE GRAND NATIONAL

The Best Horse Race In The World. The horses have to jump over fences that are so big and difficult that quite often some of them die. Die! That never happens at the show jumping, does it (although we are the best at that, too)? No, there, at your Badminton Horse Trials the fences are all exactly the height a horse can manage comfortably, but at the Grand National they are made of hedges with random spiky bits sticking out of them, that can stab the horses, and then they fall into a ditch where they can drown. It doesn't happen every year, but it's worth watching just in case it does. That's why the Grand National is The Best Horse Race In The World. Along with the Derby.

THE TOUR DE[32] FRANCE

The Best Cycling Race In The World. Even though most of it takes place in France, it's just passing by in the background and is consequently blurred for most of the time. They realised, the French organisers, that the Tour de France was never going to achieve full and proper recognition as the best cycling race in the

[31] Forty-Euro French words.
[32] Forty-Euro French word.

world unless it took place in Britain. So they changed the route – turned a few arrows round, stuck up some new ones with *Bleu-Tac* – so that all the cyclists cycled into a train station, up onto the platform, straight onto the Eurostar, and then raced around Kent, the Beer Garden of England, for a bit. It wasn't the fastest bit of the race, on account of all the cyclists sitting up and looking around, going: 'Cor! This is better, isn't it? Some proper bloody countryside for a change!', but it was the best. Fact is, we don't even have a cycling race ourselves. We're not that bothered about it. It's more of a French thing, like *boules*, runny cheese and ignominious military defeat.

THE BRITISH OPEN

The Best Golf Tournament In The World. There are four major tournaments in the world of golf, and the other three are all in America, but you ask any golfer in the world, no matter which

The kilt was invented purely to find out what degrading clothing an American would wear to win the British Open.

country he comes from, which golf tournament he wants to win the most, and he'll tell you. Our one. Because it's the best. The Yanks will try anything to have the best golf tournament. They even give out special green jackets to the winners, which is just lame – these guys make so much money they can wear anything they like. Our Open is played at a different golf course every time, which makes it ferociously difficult for the top golfers, who are very superstitious and like to have the same hotel room every year – that penthouse suite near Wentworth might be very nice, but not much use when the Open's at Carnoustie, mate.

THE SIX NATIONS

The Best Rugby Union Competition In The World. This is in effect to determine which is the best rugby team in the Northern Hemisphere. Six Nations take part in this – the clue's in the name – and four of them are British, to wit: Us, The Jocks, The Taffs and The Micks. The Southern Hemisphere have their own thing, the Tri-Nations, it's called. Only Three Nations in that, so it's naturally only half as good.

THE BRITISH BROADCASTING CORPORATION

The Best Broadcasting Corporation In The World. Especially when it comes to sports. Just look at when we have to watch coverage that American telly has provided and you'll see all the faces are too yellow, and all the people in the crowd are distorted so that they seem grossly overweight. And when SKY do the cricket we see more shots of girls in bikinis bouncing around than we do of the batsmen. The BBC know how to cover sports properly. Years of experience means they know exactly what tinkly music to put over arty camera shots of the rain spattering off the covers at Wimbledon, or Lord's, or off the roof of the stand at Twickenham.

Everyone thought Des Lynam was the best sports broadcaster in the world when he was at the BBC, and then he upped sticks and went to ITV, following in the footsteps of Mike Yarwood, Morecambe and Wise and Sooty – insofar as Sooty can be said to have footsteps – and everyone was shocked at first, because they thought maybe Des knew something, maybe ITV were finally going to get it right, but it turned out it was just the beginning of a slippery slope that was eventually to lead him to *Countdown*.

And the BBC do radio too. The British have a World Service because we run the world. The French have a Foreign Legion, because they run away from the world.

Just steer clear of the phone-ins.

RUDYARD KIPLING (1865-1936)

writer, said

*'East is east, and west is west,
and ne'er the twain shall meet.'*

Bollocks. They're going to meet in the middle, aren't they, near Birmingham somewhere. Didn't think it through, did you, Rudyard? And what sort of a name is Rudyard, anyway? Did your dad think it would make you sound tough, give you a head start in the playground? 'Ooh, here comes Softie Simpkins, let's nick his tuck money. Oh, hang on, he's with Rudyard Kipling, better not.' If your dad was hoping for a hard case he's got to have been disappointed when you decided to go into the cake business.

WE DON'T NEED NO
HEDUCATION[33]

Hey! Teacher! Leave them kids alone! Seriously, it's not worth the candle. Fat birds in shell-suits chucking bricks through your window, not daring to pop out for a paper. There's got to be a better way.

Teachers – and I'm generalising here but it is my book so back off – are a bunch of pot-smoking ecstasy-gobbling caners at best, who complain about how much marking they have to do but then have six weeks off in the summer. Chancers.

School. The point of school should be to set you up, so you can go and earn a crust, but if you don't know what you want to do, then how do they know what to teach you? It goes against all Common Sense. In the olden days, you would just do exactly what your dad did: if he was a blacksmith, then it was good enough for you and rightly so. My old man was a Publican, he taught me everything I needed to know and little else, and that's fine by me.

The only school I've got any time for is the School Of Hard Knocks, which is all about learning on the job. When you've got your sleeves rolled up unblocking the sit-down in the gents for the third time that week up to your elbows in cack AGAIN!

[33] Of course this is grammatically incorrect and means we do need education but the lad at the publishers told me to think of some snappy titles. I thought Pink Floyd were supposed to be clever anyway, you don't hear Queen singing 'I don't not want to not break free' do you?

because the chef has made too thick a mix for the Yorkshire puddings, trust me you'll be grateful you're not sat in some library somewhere reading bloody poems.

Then, if you really feel the need for further education, you can graduate to the University Of Life. Non-accredited, free, hard as nails, sharp as a tack: the time honoured system of Learn And Error, the Academy of Common Sense. There's no one telling you what you should and shouldn't know, because you just learn it, you pick it up as you go along, not like some lah-di-dah lecturer offering his latest opinion on whatever it is the *Guardian* have told him to apologise for this week. At real college you read about stuff, write it down, read about it, write it down, read about it, write it down, read about it, write it down, read about it, write it down, read about it, write it down, read about it, write it down, read about it, write it down, read about it, write it down, read about it, write it down, read about it, write it down: oh you've looked it up, but have you actually done it? NO!!

Thank God you're reading this book eh?

MATHS – YOU'LL NEVER NEED IT

Never have got along with maths. Thank God for the till they've sorted for us. Finally the brewery getting something right.

I don't mind sums, but when we get onto long division I am lost. I don't remember a thing about that, and I'm not going to sit here and strain my brain to work out how on earth long division might work. But there's this whole field of maths that seems totally pointless – apart from VAT calculations – the whole 'Ah but do numbers really exist' business, 'What is two? What is it?', the kind of question maths students spend three years at university figuring out to no apparent purpose. We had a maths student work the bar for a while and he was hopeless – quadratic equations don't help when it's pints, wines and bar snacks, that change won't sort itself. If I were a taxpayer – which I'm not seeing as I'm dead for tax purposes, which is totally practical right up until you need to go either to hospital or abroad – I'd be furious to think there was a bunch of Herberts sat around debating the precise nature of the number three. And as for the fools who say something along the lines of 'God's in the numbers …' no he's not, he's on a cloud upstairs somewhere, get over it (see RELIGION).

When they teach you about Algebra they say to you, 'You can't add apples to oranges', don't they? 'You can't add apples to oranges' – well, of course you can, can't you? What do you think the fruit bowl's for? Stick 'em in there with a lovely bunch of bananas – that's that, done and dusted, apples and oranges added, no problem.

But, the real worry for me is

How is that possible? A minus times a minus is a plus. I don't think so… If I ain't got no pint, I ain't got no pint end of story. Maths has nothing to do with how people live their lives. Then of course they'll tell you that numbers don't exist as such, that they aren't really there. You try telling that to your bank manager when you're broke. Apparently it's a double negative, but as far as I can tell there ain't no need to get upset about it.

HISTORY DEBUNKED

The purpose of history, so the historians tell us, is summed up in this pithy phrase: 'If you want to know where you're going, you have to look back at how you got to where you are.' Which is why historians are so easy to spot. They're the jokers walking around with cricks in their necks bumping into things. So much for history.

Truth is kids don't know any history any more, they're too busy being taught about humanities etc., etc. whatever they are. This means that every spotty Herbert who applies for a bar job at my place can't spell or figure out how to work the till. Ask a 14-year-old what 1066 means to him and he's most likely to say it's the price of a regular pizza with a side order of chicken wing dippers. Ask him if he knows who Nelson was and he'll point at you and go 'Ha ha!' like the bully in *The Simpsons*. Try to get him to tell you what happened between 1939 and 1945 and he'll say 'I don't know, it was the ad break so I wasn't watching. Did Barry Scott do a new *Cillit Bang* advert?' Not only will he not know there was a World War he won't even know who won! I feel sorry for kids today. I mean, what's a kid like that going to get out of watching *Where Eagles Dare*, eh? Exactly.

Apart from a string of famous victories over the French, what can we learn from history?

Well, we can learn that the price of things always goes up.

That empires rise and fall – which means the Yanks will get their come-uppance.

That washing your hands is a good idea.

That in the end things will get better. Or worse.

That a tie will never go out of fashion.

That someone will do the washing up, it's just a question of toughing it out.

That the Greeks were top dog, then the Romans, then the Goths, then the Francs, then the Holy Roman Empire, then the Spanish, then the English, then the British, then the Americans – and all this time there have been more Chinese than anyone else, but they haven't done anything about it. Thank God.

 Never run with scissors.[34]

 That royal families have always shagged around, princes will be princes.

 That things were better in the old days even when they were worse. Never forget there are many people who enjoyed the Blitz. Even if they can't remember it.

 That farmers can never be happy.

 That essentially federations can be made to work, but without a unity of morality, purpose and financial institutions there is no way that their long term future can be guaranteed – one only has to consider the counter-tension of forces within the United States of America that ran as an undercurrent for the first half of the 19th century to realise that incompatible cultural notions and aspirations can only lead to catastrophic political crisis and possibly war – the USA had to be welded together violently with a greater loss of life in that one war than in all wars that the US has since participated in. Which is why you can only really have your doubts about the EU.

[34] Did you know there's no **German** word for running with scissors

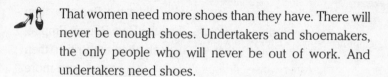 That women need more shoes than they have. There will never be enough shoes. Undertakers and shoemakers, the only people who will never be out of work. And undertakers need shoes.

There will never be enough shoes. That's a universal constant. There has to be at least one more pair of shoes per woman than the number of shoes that each woman has. In fact if you need to define infinity that's as good as a way as any – the number of shoes that would satisfy womankind.

Mathematicians say that there is no such thing as infinity plus one, that that number would be infinity itself. Well I can't agree – infinity plus one is the number of shoes required by the world's female population. You do the sums – it's infinity plus one. Or strictly speaking infinity plus two.

The Common Sense History Quiz

Anyway, here's a little history quiz for you (they don't teach any of this stuff any more):

1) Who won World War One? *We did* ✓

2) Who won World War Two? *We did* ✓

3) Who won the Falklands War? *We did* ✓

4) Who won Gulf War 1? *We did* ✓

5) Who won Gulf War 2 (This Time It's Personal)? *We did* ✓

6) Who won the Napoleonic War? *We did* ✓

7) Who won the Boer War? *We did* **WELL DONE!**

8) Who won the Spanish War of Succession? *We did* ✓

9) Who won the Seven Years War? *We did* ✓

10) Who won the American War of Independence? *We did* ✓

We could see how the bastards were going to turn out and wisely decided we'd be better off without them.

10/10

History is written by the winners. French history books are blank from cover to cover.

AH, MISTER BOND,
I'VE BEEN EXPECTING YOU...

One topic that's bound to heat things up on a quiet night in the pub, or any night when there's a Bond film on the telly, which is something like four nights a week if you've got the digital, is this: which is the best Bond? Best Bond, best film, best villain, best bird: the debate can meander down a number of different paths, everyone has their favourites.

One thing which is beyond dispute, however, is that this is an area in which you cannot afford to find yourself uninformed, so read the following carefully, commit to memory, then eat it to prevent it from falling into the hands of enemy agents, Meester Bond! (I'm joking, of course, there's no need to eat it – that will only ruin a perfectly good book and reduce its resale value. Just scribble it out with a biro.)

What we're talking about here is proper Bonds by the way. Everyone knows that the first Bond was a Yank on telly called Barry Nelson who played him as a Yank in a version of Casino Royale and that Bob Holness[35] played him on the radio. Everyone who's ever done a pub quiz knows that, so I won't be wasting your valuable and precious time with those two Herberts.

---

[35] You wouldn't have thought it, would you? But think about it: Goldfinger, Goldeneye, Gold Run – there's a theme running through the whole thing. Holness played Bond in a 1956 South African radio serial version, before there were ever any Bond films. Good job it was on the radio, really, because if they'd been able to see him, the smiley grey-haired old geezer, no one would ever have taken him seriously.

The Bond line up is as follows:

THE ORIGINAL AND BEST: SCOTTISH BOND

🍸🍸🍸🍸🍸

James Bond is the quintessential[36] Englishman. Except in his choice of drink, that is. Vodka Martini, shaken not stirred, I ask you. He'll have a pint, and behave himself, and if he comes in with Pussy Galore then she'll have a glass of white wine or a fruit-based drink, whatever her bedroom preferences may be. If he asks nicely he can have a couple of olives in his pint – he is James Bond, after all, I don't want it to kick off, I might get shot. This is the thing about Bond that you have to remember when weighing up your Bonds – he has a licence to kill, and when you watch the films you have to ask yourself: would this man kill you?

I have a licence to sell intoxicating liquors on these premises, so I too could kill you.

Naturally, given that they were looking for a quintessential Englishman, they gave the job to a Scotsman. A Scotsman, what's more, who says 'Yesh' when he means 'Yes', and 'Thish' when he means 'This', and who votes for Shcotland to be a sheparate country – as if they'd last a minute on their own now we've spent all their oil money – even though the Queen gave him a knighthood out of the goodness of her heart. There's bloody gratitude for you. And let's not forget he lives in a sheparate country to Scotland.

Sean Connery, the Scottish Bond, was the first film Bond, and the one against which all the others have to be measured. You really

[36] £40 word

72

got the feeling he could kill you. He was really good at all kinds of fighting, including: train fighting *(From Russia With Love)*, hat fighting *(Goldfinger)*, underwater fighting *(Thunderball)*, and Japanese stick fighting, especially when the other guy had a knife hidden in his stick *(You Only Live Twice)*. And he was versatile: he disguised himself as Japanese by squinting, punching women, and flying around with a rocketpack on. This was proper honest to goodness psychopathic secret agent stuff.

He's pissed and he's got a gun.

Scottish Bond was so sexy (I was never confused) that he was the only one to have the distinction of actually curing a confirmed lesbian, in *Goldfinger*, and he was a cold-blooded and ruthless assassin to boot. Who can forget, in *Dr No*, where he lies in wait for a killer, playing patience, having stuffed a bed full of pillows so it looks like he's asleep, (which is a bit of a *Famous Five* idea, really), and he says, cool as you like:

'That'sh a Shmith and Wesshon, Professhor, and you've had your shixsh ...'

And then he shoots the bloke, double tap, execution-style. Although he didn't need to because the guy had already drowned in Connery's spittle.

Connery is the original and best Bond: even though the colour's funny in those films and the gadgets got more gadgety, he's top of the shop, number 1. Really, when he quit they should have thrown in the towel.

ENGLISH BOND (1): NIVEN SAY NIVEN AGAIN

🔫🔫🔫🔫🔫

The first English Bond was David Niven, in *Casino Royale*. Broadly similar in style and approach to David Niven in *The Pink Panther*, i.e., he was posh, had a head like a walnut with a little moustache and he looked too old for the skiing. The only good thing about this whole misbegotten

episode is that it's useful to have up your sleeve for pub quiz purposes. *Casino Royale* was a spoof of the other Bond films, and it's a pretty shabby effort really. It featured, if memory serves, people hiding inside suits of armour, which only actually works in *Scooby Doo*. One of those films that makes you realise how long Sunday afternoons can be.

AUSTRALIAN BOND: 'G'DAY BLOFELD!'

Quite frankly, I don't know where to look.

When Connery decided he'd had enough of being Scottish Bond, saying, as legend has it, 'Never again!' (only to reappear in *Never Say Never Again* with Mr Bean), the mantle passed to George Lazenby, who was an Australian[37] male model out of an advert for chocolates. And then they were surprised how he turned

[37] Proof the world's a topsy turvy place: he should have been serving the Martinis, not quaffing them.

74

out. He looked good in a tuxedo, and a kilt, and when walking along or doing the skiing, but pretty much whenever he opened his mouth you wished he hadn't. Still, even though he was the worst Bond, and they only let him do the one film, *On Her Majesty's Secret Service*, it turned out to be one of the best, owing to something called the Lazenby Paradox. And the fact that it had Emma Peel in it, and Kojak, and Inspector Wexford. And Joanna Lumley, and Jenny Hanley off of *Magpie*.

ENGLISH BOND (2): MOORE IS MORE

The second English Bond, and the second one to be knighted (so far: Holness gets slightly less optimistic every time a New Year's Honours List goes by). Connery came back after Lazenby to do *Diamonds Are Forever* – 'right idea, Mister Bond, wrong pussy' – but then packed it in again because he was too old. Then they got Roger Moore off *The Persuaders*, who was even older. They really hadn't thought it through. Roger was always too old, even at the beginning, when his trouser waistbands were so high that he looked like he was always wearing a cummerbund. Even with a swimming costume.

Roger's speciality was sitting in a Winnebago somewhere eating mashed up fruit and biscuits while his costumes went climbing mountains, or parasailing, or deep sea diving. He kept the series going, though, bless him, as they were able to make significant budget savings by making his hair and his safari jackets out of the same material.

This was the period when Bond was funny, and as well as being equipped with the latest hi-tech gadgets, Roger seemed to have a

brilliant, pithy one-liner ready for every eventuality. 'He's dead tired!' – he's not dead tired, he's dead. Pay attention. You stuck his neck in a hay baler. In the end you got the feeling that Bond was killing people in unusual ways simply to help the gags he'd prepared earlier get as many laughs as possible.

This Bond was also frequently pitted against improbable giants who were half made of metal – metal arms, metal teeth – and who would be completely unaffected by Roger's best and hardest punch. Then they would smile, metallically, and Roger would take a deep breath and try again. Good luck with that, mate. This was the only Bond you could trap in a wet paper bag and be reasonably sure he'd still be there when you came back from taking over the world.

It's every man's dream to disappoint two women at once.

They tried their hardest to make Bond seem young during Roger's tenure. The theme tunes were done by ever younger and younger people – McCartney, Sheena Easton, even Duran Duran, God help us – and they'd always pit him against another old timer, like Christopher Lee, or give him a really crumbly sidekick, like Steed out of *The Avengers*, or good old 'Q', but eventually the British theatre simply ran out of actors venerable enough to zimmer it out with him and he had to go.

He had some good bits, though, no question. The false superfluous third nipple, of course, and the car that drives underwater and shoots rockets up at hovering helicopters – always handy, especially if you've knocked a few pints back and want to get home via the canal to avoid speed traps. But at no point did you get the feeling that he would kill you.

WELSH BOND: LICENCE TO KILL

This lad, Tim Dalton, is also known as Proper Actor Bond. The thinking here was that the Yanks are always massively over-impressed by British actors who've 'done a bit of theatre'. Look at Dame Judi, who also crops up in these a bit later as M. She's the same in everything, a punchy little pug dog with a prison haircut, but she's only got to turn up and they're chucking awards at her like they're dog biscuits. It's like the Yanks can't believe she's never had a facelift and so they reckon there must be something bloody clever going on that they're not bright enough to get.

Now, the trouble with Dalton was his acting was so good that he hardly even opened his mouth when he was talking, and never ever smiled, not even when the big villain got burned up by the spillage from a petrol tanker (with drugs in it). Another thing: he looked exactly like Robert Pires, who used to play for Arsenal, and who is French. Still, he did ride down a mountain on a cello case, so it wasn't all a write off. You got the feeling that he might kill you, but that he'd be happier doing it wearing tights and a ruff and running you through with a sword.

He's pissed and he hasn't got a gun. But he might get someone with passive smoking.

IRISH BOND: PETE BROSNAN

🔫🔫🔫🔫🔫

After Scottish Bond, English Bond and Welsh Bond, they had to go for an Irish one next to get their card stamped. It really reduced their options, though, and in my view it was political correctness gone mad. In the end, apparently, it came down to a choice between yer man Brosnan and Terry Wogan, which frankly was a narrow escape for all concerned. Imagine Wogan catches up with the big villain, sits him down for a nice chat, touches his knee and says: 'So tell me, after you've taken over the world, what's next for you...?'

Pete Brosnan made a decent Bond in my view. Bit of a throwback to the second English Bond, in some ways, although, unlike Moore, Brosnan himself is an ageless freak boy-man, in the mould of a Donny Osmond, and you could see him doing the part well into his eighties. You could sense the relief all round that at last Bond could be pitted against some opponents who still had all their own teeth, like Sean Bean who was *Sharpe* in *Sharpe*, or Robert Carlyle off of TV's *Hamish Macbeth*. Even so, no matter how young the villain is he still calls the girl 'My dear', like he's her grandad or something. That's how you can tell he's the villain. Don't mess with the formula. Though it has to be said that there's no way Pete would kill you, though if he did he'd probably do it half like Roger Moore, half like Sean Connery, which I suppose was the point, really.

He's sober and he's got a gun

78

HARD AS NAILS BOND: SHARP AS A TACK

🔫🔫🔫🔫🔫

In a way you get the Bonds you deserve,
and Hard As Nails Bond, or English Bond
(3), has a bit of a funny face, in my view.
The ladies are meant to be swooning, but
for me there's a strange Hallowe'en mask
quality about the features which gives the
character an enigmatic cast. Now, this
latest Bond film is meant to bring the
whole thing full circle. For a start, it's
Casino Royale, again, but not a spoof like

I was never confused

before. In fact this one's played dead straight, they've throttled back
on the gadgets a bit – although he does have an electric jump
starter for his heart in the glove compartment of his car, at least the
car is not remote-controlled *(Tomorrow Never Dies)* or completely
invisible[38] *(Die Another Day)*.

And the iconic scene where Ursula Andress emerges from the
waves in a white bikini is revisited, as is the iconic scene where
Halle Berry emerges from the waves in an orange bikini, except
it's Daniel bloody Craig emerging from the waves in a pair of
pale blue boxer shorts! How is that the same? What am I
supposed to get out of that? I was never confused...

BOOK BOND

Worth a mention I guess, but it has to be said that that Ian
Fleming bloke they got in to write the movie tie-in books did a

[38] Of all the cheap special effects a car that isn't there has to take the biscuit.

woeful bloody job. I picked up a copy of Moonraker in Oxfam the other day and it has to be said I'm not sure that Mr Fleming has even seen the film! There's no Jaws in it, in fact Bond doesn't even go into space. Terrible effort. I wouldn't bother buying them if I were you.

CONCLUSION

So, there you are then, the complete Bond overview, for if that ever comes up in the pub. There's no need to thank me – the £18.99 you paid to purchase this book is thanks enough.

And Tom Baker is the best Dr Who too. (See *DR WHO: WHO'S BETTER WHO'S BETTER WHO'S BEST?*)

RENE DESCARTES (1596-1650)
French philosopher, said

'I think, therefore I am.'

I think, therefore I am what, Rene? Not only have you not thought it through, you haven't finished your sentence. I think, therefore I am awake. That's the insight in full, I believe. I think, therefore I am awake. I do not think, therefore I am asleep, or else pissed, or acting while the balance of my mind is disturbed. Typical Frenchman, knocking off early. He's probably got as far as: 'I think, therefore I am …' and thought, that'll do me for the morning, I'm off to the café for a Ricard and some brie in a baguette. An Englishman will finish the job for me. Second World War – exact same story.

SHAKESPEARE

AND WHY YOU REALLY SHOULDN'T
WORRY ABOUT HIM

Not all he's cracked up to be.

Shakespeare eh? The cornerstone of all literature and the greatest writer what the world has ever known – so we are told. His quotes are the immortal quotes of the English language bla bla etc., etc. We should just be grateful to be talking the same language as the long dead bald fella.

YOU'VE HEARD ALL THIS STUFF BEFORE.[39]

[39] We really must have a theatre where the plays that no one likes and no one has seen are on 24 hours a day if only to fleece passing Yanks who don't know better.

His plays, we are told, offer us fabulous insight into the human condition (the human condition right here right now is a sore throat and a dull sense of regret about some of the things I think I said last night but I'm not sure whether I really said them or not and it would probably be for the best if I hadn't, but them's the breaks when you get into the whisky and frankly I have no idea what possible insight Shakey could have into that).

Anyway, let's rehearse our Common Sense arguments against the Bard of Boredom.

Point the first: Shakespeare does not talk the same language as you and me: forsooths, gadzooks and a bare bodkin. If you want the man on the street and the woman in the home to be able to relate to this stuff you're going to have to sort this out.

Point the second: How can a play about an indecisive Danish prince possibly have any bearing on the day to day running of a not-as-busy-as-it-could-be-pub?

Point the third: Macbeth – lots of Scots knifing each other. So the obvious counts as fabulous insight does it?

Point the fourth: If these plays are so good, why aren't they on telly all the time, instead of *Wild At Heart*?

Point the fifth: Tights. I was never confused.

SO THAT JUST ABOUT SUMS IT UP: YOU REALLY SHOULDN'T WORRY ABOUT SHAKESPEARE.

Mind you, bloke from the Midlands, writing poetry, he'd have been as hard as nails, handy man on the pub football team. **What a waste.**

IS MY PUB A WINE BAR?
PART 1

People – by which I mean people who don't drink in my pub – are always asking me one question:

'Guvnor?' they say, 'I am worried, I cannot sleep at night.'

'What is it?' I reply.

'I am concerned,' they go on, a tear beginning to sprout in the corner of either eye. 'I am concerned that my pub [by which they mean the pub they drink in instead of drinking in mine] may be a wine bar. How can I tell?'

I then manfully resist the temptation to say, 'Come and drink in my pub, which is a pub – problem solved, you tear-stained loser!'

And introduce them to my simple checklist, which I have arrived at by applying my British brain and my years of experience chipping away at the beer face.

CHECK FOR PUB BASICS

This is really straightforward. Just go into your pub, or, as it may be, wine bar, and check off these basic features. A child could do it of course. It couldn't then go on and purchase an alcoholic beverage, that's more than my livelihood's worth. The mystery customer might be in.

THE LANDLORD

This bloke owns the place (or in my case runs it for the bastard brewery. Leave that bit out they might read it especially if it's early on in the book) and therefore you should treat him with total and utter respect, even when he's had far too much to drink and gets lairy, which due to the stresses and strains of the job can sometimes happen especially when, say, the wife leaves for France with his boy the same night he's found out the brewery know all about his illegal fruit machine. Remember he can bar you and you can't bar him.

Landlords by their very nature are incredibly wise and intelligent people due to their line of work, [40] – coming into contact with every type of person means they need to be able to talk every kind of talk. They will be told things by people the wrong side of seven pints – things that they really shouldn't know, secrets of the highest regards.

Come on Mr Porky, this has got to be worth a couple of free boxes.

[40] (See the honourable order of publicans.)

I learned my trade at the Landlord Academy for seven years, but they didn't tell me anything I didn't know before. Besides I failed my finals and I can still pull a round, change a barrel and in a blind taste test, tell the difference between Mr Porky's and Tavern Snacks Pork Scratchings.

If your pub is a wine bar it will not have one of these. It will have a Manager. He will be younger than you, will recently have graduated from a catering college, and will have no time to stop and listen to your tales of woe and how the world has ground you down just a little bit further this week. He is too busy thinking about the mark up on a bottle of Berschlisselhimmler, beer of the Black Forest.

THE BAR STAFF

While the Landlord is fulfilling his core function, providing a still hub of Common Sense around which Pub Life can revolve, someone has to pull the pints, mop up the spillages, tot up the small change, and make sure the Lifeboat-shaped collecting tin doesn't go walkabout.

In many beautiful British pubs nowadays these people are Australians, who are genetically engineered for bar work. The males have a happy-go-lucky attitude which puts your regulars at their ease, and it's possible to negotiate a deal whereby you pay them exclusively in beer. The female of the species is similarly blessed, with the additional advantage that she will more than likely be tanned and attractive, or at least tanned, and thus will act as an exotic light to the punter's moth, so to speak. That's not meant to be rude, it's poetical.

The point of this is to keep the mugs there drinking, in the hope that maybe, just maybe, there's a remote chance of some action. Sadly though, an immutable Law of Nature says that the more beer the punters have the less attractive they become, while the barmaid's attractiveness through the eyes of said punters increases correspondingly until she becomes the most beautiful and frustratingly unobtainable woman alive…and so the dance of life – and the drinking – continues. (See *LIFE'S GREATEST JOKES OF ALL.*)

If your pub is a wine bar, the bar staff will give you your change on a little saucer with a till receipt, and look pissed off if you don't let them keep it as a tip, even though you've had to get up from your table and go over to the bar to get served and they've just stood there looking snotty and sniggering at your attempts to pronounce whatever is the closest approximation to a decent British pint they offer.

REGULARS

One day, if you are particularly blessed, you may be vouchsafed the title of 'regular' in a Beautiful British Pub. You will have your own favourite seat or, more likely, stool, from which you will discern titbits, such as on which nights the tastiest barmaid works. You will learn not to eat the food, excepting pre-wrapped bar snacks manufactured off the premises. Most importantly you will be able to go in on your own and not be by yourself, you will know the other regulars and they will know you, you'll be able to sit at the bar, and on those golden evenings when the Guv'nor feels like having a lock in you will be one of the chosen few that is ushered into the function room while he clears the other riff raff out. However it's not all take take take: you must be loyal in return, and if you leave it longer than three months without popping in, don't bother going back.

If your pub is a wine bar it will not have regulars. They pride themselves, for some reason, on their high turnover of customers. If a wine bar manager sees you more than twice in a month, he is likely to mistake you for a stalker and get some kind of a restraining order.

BLOKES GETTING THEIR ROUND IN

The ultimate pub tradition, as I'm sure you know, is Getting Your Round In. Getting Your Round In is a beautiful thing. Poetry. Truth. Proof that we are not alone, that we can affect others in this bleak, grey world. It's doing your bit, sharing your load, taking your part in the Common Weal. It is a Good Thing.

Though Good can lead to Evil. Because getting your round in is the basis of Communism. That's right: getting your round in will work with seven or eight mates, you get yours in, they get in theirs, that'll make your Friday night into a Saturday morning, but apply it to 150 million Russians and it ain't going to work. Especially if the first bloke at the bar is someone as devious and ruthless as Josef Stalin: the moment he worked out what it was going to cost him to buy 150 million pints he set about purging his fellow Russians – just to get his bar bill down! And that, that is evil, from a good idea. Hitler was never interested in getting anyone's drinks in, and that's why in the end it was inevitable that we would end up having to destroy him.

If your pub is a wine bar, you will not see blokes getting their round in. You will see losers ordering another bottle of the white and another bottle of the red, and then arguing about the bill at the end of the evening, saying things like: 'Well, I only had two glasses, so I'm only putting in a fiver...'

A DARTBOARD

The proper place for a dart board, as every landlord knows, is on the wall alongside the entrance to the gents toilet. Check there first, and if what you see is a large metal poster in the style of a Pear's soap advert from the thirties or a series of framed pictures of the Forth Road Bridge in various stages of its construction, then, my friend, you have my sympathy. Your 'pub' is a wine bar.

If, however, you see a dartboard all may be well. I have to warn you, though – drinker beware – of the creeping rise of the pub that is not a pub. Which is to say the pub that is really a wine bar, or worse, but which is hoping to be mistaken for a pub in order to chisel you, the unsuspecting drinker, out of your hard earned. In such a place, if you can believe it, a dart board may be a quisling, used to

The faithful old pincushion

throw you off your guard, and before you know it you will be quaffing ice cold bottled lager from Norway under the misguided impression that this is now *all right.*

You should also check that the plaster on the wall is pitted in a circular pattern around the edges of the dartboard, evidence of prolonged mixed-ability darting. The dartboard should be contained in a wooden box which opens out to reveal two little blackboards. These should still bear the scores of a recent game of 501, which seems to have taken at least forty darts by each player to complete. Failing that, the legend 'Gary is a twat' or similar.

If your pub is a wine bar, then asking the barman for 'a lend of the pub arrers' will cause him to look at you as though you are some kind of mentalist. And the dartboard may well be in a strange and unfamiliar colour scheme, such as blue and yellow, and have no treble ring. When asked about this, the 'landlord' will cheerfully admit that it is an antique, which he picked up on holiday in the Dordogne, and that he couldn't possibly let you play on it as you might get holes in it.

A BEER GARDEN

Taking a break from chucking bricks through windows.

The pub garden has an ancient purpose, it is where you dump your kids while you get a couple in yourself. Hence sandpits, swings (I creosote mine every year even though they're metal, it's tradition, innit?) and the rest of the beer garden accoutrements.[42] Actually, speaking from personal experience, the sandpit at my place is a nightmare. You have no idea what might be buried in there, and the thing stinks of fox-crap. One time Gary repaired a motorbike of his over by the

[42] French word.

90

sandpit and dropped the gear box in there. The thing seized permanent, naturally. When I said I wasn't paying for it, he deposited a whole sump's worth of gear oil into the sand. Disgusting. The kids don't seem to care though. Should have barred him for that, but he's a mate. At time of writing, anyway, the mad bastard...

Good beer gardens are all about summer, lager top, sunshine and pretty gels in skimpy tops...ah, they're all pretty in the summer aren't they? It's been a year.

With the introduction of the Smoking Ban the beer garden has taken on an altogether grimmer appearance; after a rainy day or two it ends up like the Somme, mud smeared, fag butts like spent cartridges, people never returning from the sodden filth and squalor, at the going down of the sun, we will remember them...

If your pub is a wine bar it will not have a beer garden. It won't really have beer, so why should it have a beer garden? It could have a wine garden, I suppose, but the chances are it's crammed in between WH Smiths and Dewhursts in a pedestrian arcade with no greenery to speak of within a radius of two or three miles. If you're lucky.

THE PUB'S NAME

This can give you a heads up right away. In fact, it would make more sense if this was the first thing on the checklist, because you could do it before you even go into the place. I just realised I haven't Thought This Through... Anyway, the important thing to remember is that proper pubs are named properly, after a small range of proper things which are proper.

These proper things are as follows: royalty past or present, for example The King, The Queen, The Prince of Wales, The King Charles, The Queen Victoria, and The Prince William (of Orange or otherwise).

The aristocracy, past or present: examples include The Marquis of Granby, The Earl of Windsor, The Duchess of Malmesbury, and The Duke of Wellington.

National heroes, past or present (but mostly past), such as Admiral Nelson, The Duke of Wellington (again), and Henry Cooper.

Parts of the body of any of the above, as in The King's Head, The Queen's Arms, The Duke of Wellington's Legs.

And finally certain robust and manly animals and parts of their bodies. I'm talking about your Bull, your Ram, your White Horse, and your Stag's Head, but not, under any circumstances, your Frog.

If your pub is a wine bar, it will have a name made up of two unrelated items yoked together in an unnatural union. Things like The Stool and Turnip, The Frog (!) and Nightgown, The Piano and Cake, or The Pizzle and Merkin. We've all seen them. We know what they are. Give them a wide berth.

The alternative is a name implying that the establishment belongs to a bloke you haven't heard of who's a lot more fun than you are. Something like Bertie's, Stan's, Hacker's, Flick's, Waldo's or Texas Pete's. Go in there if you must, but don't expect to bump into Bertie, Waldo or Texas Pete. They're round the corner in a proper pub having a beer. Laughing at you.

I hope this has been of some help to you. You should now know in your own mind whether or not your pub is a pub, or a wine bar (or even, Heaven help you, something worse).

If, however, you are still quivering with uncertainty, it may be time to move onto something a little more advanced.

See *IS MY PUB A WINE BAR PART 2*

QUESTIONS BEST LEFT UNASKED

#3

'It's been a while since I bought you any clothes, darling – I know you were a twelve but what are you now?'

WHY THE SUPERMARINE SPITFIRE MKS1-26 IS THE GREATEST FIGHTER AIRCRAFT THE WORLD HAS EVER KNOWN AND WE SHOULD ALL BE GRATEFUL

It is. No argument.

The Supermarine Spitfire was a major breakthrough in monoplane metal fuselage single aircraft design. Designed by Reginald Mitchell from Stoke-On-Trent,[43] the Spitfire had its origins in the Schneider Trophy, a competition for boatplanes. Mitchell took his flying boat designs back to the drawing board and came up with the Spitfire – powered by a Rolls Royce Merlin engine, and with its iconic elliptical wing the Spitfire (along with its less fabled stable mate, the Hurricane) became symbolic of Britain's struggle in the Battle of Britain.

Towards the end of the 1930s it had become clear that war was a likelihood, and that existing biplane fighter aircraft design was becoming rapidly outmoded. The British government was looking for fighter aircraft designs, principally to defend the country from the perceived bomber threat. At this time defence experts had convinced politicians and the public at large that 'the bomber would always get through', so the Chamberlain government went looking for manufacturers to deliver something that could deal with this

[43] Though unlike Stoke's other favourite son, Robbie Williams, Mitchell never felt he had to claim he'd done a trial for Stoke FC in order to look cool.

threat. The two most successful tenders were from Sidney Cam's Hawker, the Hawker Hurricane, a monoplane, also powered by the Merlin, but made with a fabric-covered fuselage, and the Supermarine Spitfire, offered by parent company Vickers. Mitchell himself was gravely ill and died before he saw the Spitfire enter service.

The Battle of Britain saw both of these aircraft make their mark on history, but because the Spitfire was a more radically modern design, having a stronger airframe and higher performance, the Hurricane faded from service, and the Spitfire became the mainstay of the RAF. The sheer adaptability of the airframe's design made itself clear early on, with an aircraft carrier version the Seafire, ground attack versions, desert versions, high altitude photo reconnaissance versions, twin seater trainer versions: basically the Spitfire could do it, whatever it was.

As the war progressed different challenges presented themselves. For instance, in 1941 the Germans introduced a new fighter, the Focke Wulf FW 190. This represented a major breakthrough in German fighter design, it was much faster, more manoeuvrable, and had a better rate of climb than the Spitfire's old Battle of Britain rival the Messerschmitt BF109. The Spitfire was left temporarily vulnerable; until Supermarine turned around a new mark, with a more powerful engine; but more importantly, it was an upgrade that they could do to existing airframes. Once again the RAF gained the edge.

Throughout the Second World War the Spitfire was seen in the skies over every theatre of war: the siege of Malta, the Battle of El Alamein, the D-Day landings; wherever there were fighters, there were Spitfires. Pilots waxed lyrical about what a beautiful aeroplane it was to fly, the perfect combination of form and function. Though the Spitfire went through some 26 different marks, many in response to German innovations, it remained true to its essential design, and to this day is a symbol of the unique and poetic struggle over the skies in the fateful summer of 1940.

Frankly you ought to know this stuff and it's doing my head in to have to go over these basic British facts that every man, woman and child really should have at their fingertips at all times. What's next?

☞ **THE WAY THINGS ARE**

No. 2: You Can't Help But Look

Like the way that no matter how often you wipe your backside – and for most of us it's once a day, isn't it mate, eh? – We still have a bloody good look, don't we? What do we expect, roses? Gold leaf? It's just the way things are.

UNBEATABLE WIPING ACTION

CHEAP!

GLOBAL WARMING: DO YOUR BIT

If I understand this properly, and I think I do what with the clue being in the name, then pretty soon it's going to get a whole lot warmer. Globally. Even though it pains me to end up agreeing with the sort of people who normally wave placards[44] and want to stroke dolphins. Grow up.

Basically the Arctic ice pack is melting away in great chunks. Now this means the chances of a Titanic style disaster are greatly

[44] Oi! Swampy! Is that placard bio-degradable? Shame on you!

reduced, and it must surely mean there's more water for Africa, but what will happen is that sea level is going to rise by anything up to six feet in the not too distant. This will mean that most of Holland and Belgium will disappear under water from whence they came, along with large parts of East Anglia.

I know, I know, you're sat there scratching your head and wondering in that Common Sense way: what's the down side?

It's bad news for the Channel Tunnel, for a start. The English Channel, our trusty old exclusion zone, which has kept both Frenchmen and rabies (same difference) at bay for centuries, will virtually double in width as half of Kent and the northern French lowlands disappear under water. This means that the Chunnel, instead of going as it does now between England and France,

The Arctic (white bits not melted yet, big blue bit melted)

will go from one underwater part of the sea to another underwater part of the sea, and what's more will be filled up with sea, so it will be no use to anyone. It's going to add at least six hours to the booze run however you look at it, but also slow down any future French invasion fleet – they've been too quiet for too long!

The real nightmare scenario, though, the one that's been keeping me awake nights, is this: our fascinating, beloved, changeable climate is currently known as Temperate, because you never know what the weather's going to be like, so you're always losing your temper at it. Under the new climate regime we are going to be forcibly reclassified, without so much as a by-your-leave (whatever that is), re-zoned, if you like, because the Temperate Zone is heading northwards, and will henceforth cover Iceland, Norway and the Outer Hebrides. Our new climate zone, my friends, the new classification of Her Majesty's Kingdom of Great Britain and the United Kingdom, is to be (sit yourself down, this one's a shocker)...*gah!*...Mediterranean.

It's no use complaining to your MP. It's no use having a go at Brussels, even, because Brussels will be underneath the salty blue North Sea. Fair play. Every cloud.

Now some might say that in this respect our timing's perfect. After all, we've scarred this world with railways and small pox, set up the finest holiday locations in the world, put in airports, gift shops, the English language and trial by jury into pretty much everywhere worth going, so surely we deserve a break, time to put our feet up. After all, the Greeks, they've had their feet up for something like two and half thousand years, but fair enough, they'd done their bit, mathematics, philosophy, astronomy, democracy, the kebab: put your feet up Spiros, you've earned it.

But, if climate change is allowed to continue unchecked, we will overnight become a Mediterranean nation, an unnatural hybrid of Spain, France, Italy and Greece. How is that going to work? Well, I'll tell you.

There'll be Premier League bullfighting on the satellite for a start off, and hitmen running around all over the place pinching ladies' bottoms. Our new national drink will taste like aniseed balls, we'll be driving on the wrong side of the road, surrendering at the merest hint of international conflict, sleeping all bloody afternoon, and eating garlic cooked in olive oil and feta cheese toasties.

Worst of all, though, all the pubs will have to become pavement cafés, where old blokes in braces with one single remaining brown tooth will play chess and drink cappucino all day. Which means muggins here is going to have to splash out for a striped awning and some garden furniture, and I might even have to move the whole bloody pub because at the moment it's nowhere near the sodding pavement. And coupled with the fact that everyone will be driving on the wrong side of the road and in a state of panic and chaos, there's every chance that folks sat out on the pavement will be mown down by drivers losing the plot in the heat and all. It'll be carnage. That's nage involving a car.

So what can be done to prevent this from happening?

The root of the problem as I understand it – and when this bit came on the news the other day I have to admit there was quite a racket going on in my gaff, on account of Gary having a row with a salesman who'd blundered into an argument by mistake about which was the best surviving Beatle,[45] but I'm pretty sure I got the gist of it – is that the ozone layer in the sky is being depleted because we are all using our arseholes too much.

I know, it sounds incredible, but if we can all learn to hold it in just a couple of extra hours a day, it could make all the difference. So come on – clench for your country. You don't want this scepter'd isle to become SPA-FR-ITAL-EECE, do you?! They said something about recycling as well, but I'm not doing that, I don't care how bad things get, not since Britvic changed their bottle and got rid of the deposit system.

[45] Ringo, by the way.

BILL SHANKLY (1913-1981)
football manager, said

*'Football isn't a matter of life and death.
It's more important than that.'*

Bill Shankly's dead. I wonder which he thinks is the most important now. Football, or life and
death. Didn't think it through, did he? Poor old Shanks, you see, he was desperate to make his
mark. Didn't want to be known only as a bloke who had a pony. What sort of epitaph is that?

IS MY PUB A WINE BAR?
PART 2

All right. You've checked for the basics, and you've tried the dart board test, which has proved inconclusive. It usually does. It's not a very good test. Let's move on to the second item on my checklist.

Now let me be perfectly clear. I have nothing against wine. Pubs are, after all, obliged to stock it in case a lady comes in who is unable to enjoy a fruit-based drink for some reason, perhaps owing to a medical condition or an allergy.

The wine bar, though, takes the principle of 'ladies first' and elevates it to the status of a lunatic fringe religion. It's all very well to take care of the ladies, of course it is. Open doors by all means, offer seats on buses if you will, throw your capes into puddles with cheerful abandon. But to make their drink of choice the be-all and end-all of a whole drinking establishment, while the gentleman has to make do with bottled beer, which is invariably **German**,[46] well, it's political correctness gone mad.

---

[46] Sometimes, you know, I think that when the end was in sight for the Third Reich, and they were passing round the cyanide tablets in that Berlin bunker, some bright spark as a final cruel joke gave the green light to 'Plan B', which was the slow and gradual invasion of this country over a sixty-plus year timescale via the medium of bottled beer and luxury cars.

If you really want to know whether your 'pub' is a pub, or a wine bar, then:

CHECK OUT WHAT IS ON DRAUGHT

You would think, wouldn't you, that this would be the clincher. If your 'pub' is truly a pub, it will have pumps. Course it will. Pub 101. These will generally be of dark hard wood topped with a brass vestigial nipple, polished by years of usage to a dazzling sheen, and offering a beautiful range of kegged beverages which should ideally include some, many or all of the following:

An unimpeachable local bitter (all hail to the ale)

A mild (for use in making mild and bitter)

An Australian lager brewed in Watford

Something German (I know, it sticks in the craw, but always remember that it's your choice, and if we'd lost, it wouldn't be)

A 'real' ale (called something like Old Wanger, which will be bought exclusively by blokes in glasses and pullovers, which will have bits in it, and which will smell like the airing cupboard after a homebrew explosion)

Some variation or other of that well-known and allegedly creamy thick black Irish concoction (no names, no pack drill, for fear of reprisals – notoriously jumpy, even now, your Irish, and I'm still using my kneecaps for the foreseeable future) **in case any tourists happen to walk in.**

If your 'pub' is a wine bar then it will have no need of pumps, it will have a bottle opener. With a corkscrew on it. Or possibly some kind of Swiss Army knife. I don't know, really, it hurts me to even imagine what goes on in these places. And why on earth do the Swiss bother to have an army, let alone give them knives?

So if you enter your 'pub', and you spot a dark gleaming priapic pump handle thrusting proudly above the surface of the bar, you might be forgiven for heaving a sigh of relief. My 'pub' is a pub after all, you might say to yourself contentedly, and there's an end to the matter.

Well, no. It's not as simple as that. Things rarely are.

I tell you this, and even though I have seen these in action I can hardly believe the deviousness of the mind that thought them up. There is now on the market, and being used openly and without shame in 'pubs' up and down the country, a pump that is really a bottle opener.

Oh yes. The 'landlord' pulls on the pump handle, exactly as if he were drawing a beautiful British ale in a beautiful British pub, but down below bar level a small boy dressed in rags, his fingers raw from shelling peanuts, is removing the top from a bottle of Glöckenbolsenheimerpilsner and tipping the ungodly brew into a schooner.

Now you may say I'm being paranoid. You may say it's a beautiful idea, to allow the lowly bottled beer enthusiast to feel he is actually on a par with proper drinkers, to allow him to partake of the visceral thrill of having his beverage pulled by a qualified expert. You may say it helps the publican, too, allowing him to use exactly the same highly toned muscle groups to dispense the whole range of drinks he has to offer.

I say 'What next? A pump that dispenses draught crisps?'

It's unnatural, and the sole purpose of this devilish contraption is to sucker potential pub customers into a pub that is really a wine bar. So before you give your 'pub' the all-clear, you might want to do a quick belly-flop over the bar to check that there really are drip trays behind there and not a bottle bank. Don't worry about causing offence – any genuine self-respecting pub landlord will thank you for caring.

I trust this has been helpful so far. But a word of warning: this 'pub' of yours might have a well-worn dart board, one of those where the single twenty has inexplicably erupted in a bizarre flowering of badger hair through overuse. It could offer the widest range of draught beverages this side of the Oktoberfest, and be called The Admiral Nelson's Backside, and yet you still could not be 100 per cent sure of your ground.

See *IS MY PUB A WINE BAR PART 3*.

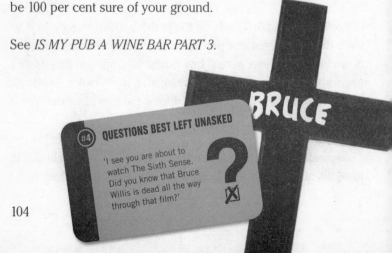

BRUCE

#4 QUESTIONS BEST LEFT UNASKED

'I see you are about to watch The Sixth Sense. Did you know that Bruce Willis is dead all the way through that film?'

BIG TOPIC NUMBER ONE: RELIGION

Why are we here? How did we get here? Where did we come from?

Questions you might ask a mini cab driver[47] when you've passed out on your way home, but also the big questions which people have sought answers for since the dawn of time. And fair enough, I reckon, when the science lot are telling you you're just a big bag of water sat on a spinning rock too tiny for anyone to notice. Sometimes you have to say, 'Oi! Lay off with the making me feel insignificant! For if we are here,[48] it must surely be for a reason, and the reason has to be more than so we can go down the pub (though don't knock it, I'm only saying there must be other reasons as well, all right?). So:

THERE IS A GOD, OBVIOUSLY, AND HE'S BRITISH, OBVIOUSLY

I believe in God. Of course I do, and not only that, I believe that he is British. Oh yes. After all we don't have earthquakes in this country do we? No, you don't shit on your own doorstep do you? The Americans, forever begging God to bless them (and I was always told it's rude to beg), have earthquakes, fat people, the international relations equivalent of bad breath as well as the

[47] Or yourself, after all he's not going to know is he. After all, he's a prince back home in Nigeria, and all he needs is £250,000 to get the bank to give him his uncle's money.
[48] Let's not get into that whole French thing of wondering whether we really are here or not, of course we bloody are.

105

world's biggest unexploded volcano lurking under the Jellystone National Park, so I'd say that there's no way he's blessed them yet. Maybe he'll get round to it, maybe he won't. If he does it'll be out of pity if nothing else, and proof that he's merciful if nothing else. God is British: there can be no arguments against it. He isn't French, is he? Of course not: or they'd be British.

CREATION

In the beginning when they realised that no one had the foggiest where they'd come from (sound familiar?) they came up with some pretty good stories to answer said questions raised. And fair play to them: they're sat in a cave or a mud hut and they haven't invented Monopoly or anything to pass the time, so who knows, a few good stories might help. So why not say that God did it, and he did the whole thing in a week? Now some might say that it's ridiculous to think the whole world was slung together in seven days, but either he's God or he's not, isn't he, eh? He can do what He likes, and He doesn't have to explain Himself, and we shouldn't even bother trying to figure Him out. That's the sort of God they came up with, and it's their story, so they get to decide.

One thing I will say about The Creation is that if you want an easy life (and who doesn't?) whatever you do don't bring it up when there's Yanks about. You'll regret it till your dying day. They've got themselves in a right lather over the whole thing, and if you open your mouth you'll be wishing you never did. You so much as raise an eyebrow about the did-it-in-seven-days story, and suddenly they'll start going on about,'Was your grandfather an ape, then?', and several of my drinkers would be deeply offended by such a remark, especially here in multi-cultural UKGB. They've gone all unnecessary, and sometimes if you get that far there's no way back, whichever creek you might be up and whatever the quotient of paddles.

BELIEFS

When you stop and look at the sort of things people believe, you realise that the world is populated by mentalists and nutters on a hitherto undreamed-of scale. Or, to put it another way, that people are, after all, only human (see *ONLY HUMAN*).

Different cultures believe all sorts of stuff. The Maoris of New Zealand believe the North Island was a giant fish hauled out of the sea by a god called Maui from his boat with a fishing rod, the boat being the South Island. How did they know that the South Island is shaped like a boat and the North Island is shaped like a fish? Eh? In the days before aerial photography, and maps? That's not really the point, though; the point is the whole thing's a bit unlikely. We put it to a vote in the snug, and our money's on plate tectonics.

The Aboriginal Australians have a thing they call the DreamTime. I haven't looked into it really, Gary thinks he knows about it, says it's something to do with a turtle dreaming things or something, but he's usually wrong. I reckon it's their equivalent of Happy Hour. But the point is it was all so long ago what is the point of arguing the toss, let alone duffing someone up over it?

And it's not just cultures: individuals believe the strangest things too. For instance, Gary believes his wife will leave her South African mercenary boyfriend with one eye and come back to him. That, in my view, makes the resurrection seem like a walk

107

in the park, a dead cert romping home Grand National winner, but I nod and agree when he gets onto the subject because some weeks, when takings are down, his misery drinking keeps us in the black. Bearing this in mind the rest is easy: you can believe whatever you like mate, and I will defend your right to believe pretty much whatever you like mate, up to the point of a nasty pub fight.

For example, the idea of Noah's Ark: some may say that fitting two of each species in the world in the Ark just wouldn't be possible, especially given the dimensions laid down in the Bible. To which I say: So what? The man did his best, which is all anyone can do, and not only that, he took his family with him. And if he ended up a few animals short, so what too? God can do whatever he likes and if it turns out they're a few insects short when the Flood ends, so what, God'll make some more. So get over it.

THE BIBLE – IT'S IN ENGLISH

There were some people a while back who claimed to have written *Happy Birthday to You*, and royalties for every time it had been sung, at least that's how I remember it. Well, it's always seemed to me that the fellas who wrote The Bible missed a trick. It's sold even more copies than *Jaws* and unlike *Jaws* you hardly ever see it dog-eared in Oxfam, yet they never got a penny.

The Bible offers pretty strong proof that God is British, seeing as it's written in English. It's a kind of English, anyway. We don't use the 'thees' and 'thous' much any more, except in *Emmerdale*. You do get these modern Bibles, though, don't you? I saw one when I stayed in that hotel on the tug-of-love snatch-back weekend. I didn't really read it, but I flicked through it in case there was a pizza menu stuck in it somewhere. The idea is that they've toned the whole thing down a bit, in case anyone should get worried by what's in there, in case the idea of eternal damnation should worry anyone and put them off going to church and affect takings at the collection. And they've got biscuits to buy.

Moses – 'Da-na!'

The Ten Commandments[19]

At the heart of The Beautiful British Bible you've got the Ten Commandments. Handed down by Moses after he was at the top of a mountain or something. The thing is they're not teaching this stuff at school any more, which the lad from the publishers tells me cuts me off from a whole demographic, but when Moses came up with these things he wasn't engaging in an exercise in niche marketing, was he?

1 Thou shalt have no other God than me etc.
Fair enough. If you'd made the lot and in seven days flat there's every chance you might get pissed off at the idea of some junior bull or frog God getting some of the credit. Lord knows, when I decorated the bathroom, tiling and everything myself and the ex started going on about what a great job we'd done I started grinding my teeth in my sleep again.

2 Thou shalt not make any false image of thy true God
But if we don't know what you look like mate, how do we know they're false images? I should have been a bloody lawyer, I tell you, though the study would cut into valuable drinking time.

3 Thou shalt not take thy Lord God's name in vain
He's three commandments into this whole thing and so far they're all about him. What kind of an ego are we dealing with here? Well the kind of ego that will send you to Hell for thinking impure thoughts, even though there's little or no chance of seeing them through on current form.

4 Keep the Sabbath holy
For once, there's no 'not', it was getting like Wayne's World wasn't it? And the Sabbath sounds good, if only it could be agreed which day we're talking about, and what we mean by holy if it's the only day you can get to Asda, well, I reckon God wants you to go Asda. He doesn't want your kids to starve, apart from the ones who are already starving, which will be part of His plan.

5 Honour your father and mother
Family, that's what it's all about.

[49] Did you know the Ten Commandments have never been translated into **German**?

b Thou shalt not murder[50]
No mention of Manslaughter As A Result Of Diminished Responsibility, sod your Health and Safety!

7 Thou shalt not commit adultery
As if I could. Somehow they manage to fit one in that points out the year-long drought this end.

8 Thou shalt not steal
What not at all? Not even pens from work? I suppose there were no pens from work in Moses' time, he didn't think it through did he?

9 Thou shalt not bear false witness against thy neighbour
Though growing a really tall Leylandii and ruining the bastard's light seems to have slipped Moses' attention, so this one gives you a fair bit of room for manoeuvre, that and hurling dog dirt over the fence. Mind you, that really has to be a last resort, in this day and age of DNA testing and all.

10 Thou shalt not covet your neighbour's house or ass
Were this an American publication there would now follow a series of sniggering remarks about asses, being the American word for arse - with this I cannot be bothered. They've paid me enough to refit the carvery for this book, and on a basic word count too, but there's no way I'm filling it up with sniggering Yankee jokes, no matter how 'well written' they may be by big teams of writers. And besides I have no idea -- and nor does anyone else in the Lounge know -- what 'covet' means. That and 'Deschew'. It came up in a crossword the other day and we couldn't think what it was, and the next day with the answers we were all baffled, God alone knows what that was doing in a The Sun quick crossword...
Most of this as you can see is common sense and all in all not a bad way to go about your day to day, and with plenty of holes in for you and me to carry on living our normal lives. Refreshingly no mention of political correctness, and unusually for something from back then, it isn't in some code predicting the end of the world or overturning everything you ever knew about the Virgin Mary. Traditionally this might be the moment to add on a couple of extra ones, but it ain't broke so I'm not going to fix it.

[50]It's a fact that cannot be denied, you're more likely to be murdered by relatives than anyone else. At Christmas. In a dispute over the remote control.

THE CHURCH OF ENGLAND

Well, this is a topic worth knocking off in just a few words. I don't go to Church on Sunday morning – I'm too busy clearing up spillages and mopping up sick, and then I have to go downstairs and clean up the pub as well – but Jesus being British means that we have a head start on getting into Heaven. Even though I think it's a fair bet no amount of forgiveness is ever going to cover me. Too bad, I'll take me porridge. How long can eternity really be...?

The Church of England is the conscience of the British people, which is why no one listens to it. Your conscience is that annoying voice that crops up just when you wish it wouldn't, in the same way that the Archbishop of Canterbury turns up on telly saying he doesn't think they should try to find a cure for something by looking, basically. Don't get me wrong, as books written in bits by blokes who never even met each other a couple of thousand years ago go The Holy Bible really isn't that bad. It covers all sorts of stuff and seems to have a lot of useful tips in case you're ever living in the desert and God keeps changing his mind about whether he likes you or not. But it's not the best guide to what to do if you've got the option on stem cell research. In fact, there's not a word on the subject.

You'd expect a bit more of the Church of England. I would, anyway. After all, it being the Church of where it is, you'd expect a healthy dash of reason and Common Sense. For instance, no one really needs to debate whether or not the Virgin Mary was a Virgin, of course she was, the clue's in the name. And anyway it doesn't matter that much. It's her personality that counts. What matters is Jesus's central message, which is: 'Love your neighbour as you love yourself', which pretty much amounts to the same as my central message, which is: 'Always get your round in'. As long as you listen to that and take it to heart, then the walking on water and the raising the dead is all pretty much flim flam.

So when a man in a mauve frock with a shepherd's crook comes on the news and starts telling me what I can and can't do in an area that plainly doesn't concern him, I turn over pronto. Which is a shame, because it being the Church of England, i.e. the Church of my country, I'd really like to like it.

Sorry mate, not interested.
Get off my telly.

JESUS – STORYTELLER SUPREME
THE PARABLE OF THE TALENTS

The Parable of the Talents is one of the great stories that Jesus told while he was telling stories during his story-telling phase. This involved him going around making points, basically, and a lot of them were good points and well made, and people would follow him around and listen. But there's one that always struck me as Jesus's own personal odyssey into tough cheese territory.

Basically the story as I remember it goes something like this: there's a dad, and he gives his two sons ten talents each, talents being money, moolah, dough, wonga, though it being one of these clever stories designed to make a point they're called talents (geddit? It's a holy pun). And he says: take care of those talents I gave you, I'm going to be away for a while, off somewhere, you don't need to know where, sons.

So son number one takes the talents and buries them at the bottom of the garden – taking care of them! Son number two heads downtown, talents in hand, and goes speculating his talents, ending up with twice as many as he started out with. Dad returns, and duffs up and generally disinherits son number one because he didn't head downtown and put his talents on a horse or whatever it was his smug brother did. You what? If Dad had said: Take care of these talents but whatever you do don't bury them at the bottom of the garden – then fair play, then the dad would have been within his rights to come down on the first like a ton of British bricks – but as it was he was bang out of order!

114

Moving the goalposts! It's an incitement to capricious parenting. Nice one Jesus. Still, nowhere near as annoying as the Return Of The Prodigal Son, which makes my bloody blood boil...

THE RETURN OF THE PRODIGAL SON

Christ, this one's annoying – and that's not a curse it's a comment addressed to the man Himself.[51] What is He playing at with this one, eh? A man has two sons (see a pattern forming, do you? Yeah, me too, and I didn't need to study literature at some lah-di-dah university to spot that one). Anyway, this man – different man, I'm presuming, or else he's really got it in for his lads – has these two sons, and one of them stays at home and works hard and does just what his dad wants him to. He does it well and grafts away, and arguably I suppose buries his talents at the bottom of the garden (although in no way does Jesus suggest there are any talents involved in this story. They're implied). The other son heads off downtown, disappears, puts his talents on the wrong horse this time and is never heard from again. Until of course he is heard from again, at which point the dad says: 'Wow! The no-good one's back!' and throws a great big feast. Meanwhile the son who's made an effort, and behaved himself, and done as he's told, has to watch as they kill the fatted calf and feed it to his no-good wastrel brother, thinking: 'I was looking forward to eating that. I've been fatting it for ages...' I forget the moral of this one, but it's basically saying something like: 'Don't do what your Dad tells you – he'll only despise you for your weakness'. Nice one Jesus. It's bloody obvious you never had kids.

[51] See THE TEN COMMANDMENTS. Number 3.

Now, I have been holding forth on the subject of the main Christian religion of this country that no one really likes or much bothers with. The fact is, though, there are loads of Gods. When Old Testament God said, 'Thou shalt have no other Gods but me',[52] these are the ones he was worried about:

Buddha, he's the fat one sitting down. You have to admire his style. If I had created the Universe complete with a system of karmic payback, which would take a great deal of paperwork if nothing else just to keep track of who's been a good dog and deserves to move up a level, I would feel I deserved a proper sit-down.

If I didn't know better that's a beer belly

[52] See THE TEN COMMANDMENTS. Number 1.

There's **Mohammed**, who ███████████████████
██ the
██ and
██ but
████████████████████████████████████, though strictly
speaking isn't the actual God, **Allah's** your chap, but
███.[53]

In India they have **Ganesh** with the elephant head and loads of spare arms. Nice stuff. I mean, if you saw that running towards you you probably would worship it, wouldn't you? Or else give him a bun. I rather like the idea of an animal-headed deity – after all, if you were a god and could do what you like, why not appear to people with an elephant's head? And tiger feet (that's neat) and a donkey's arse while you're at it?

The ancient Romans had loads of gods, owing to the fact that their Emperors and their families would suddenly discover that they were gods themselves and get themselves added to the list, so it was a bit like the system of buying knighthoods in this country nowadays. Their best god was one called **Bacchus**, the god whose sole responsibility was rolling around pissed up all the time. On wine, mostly, which is a ladies' drink of course, but even so it's an enviable divine lifestyle. If he'd been in charge of Creation it would have taken a bloody sight longer than seven days, I guarantee you that.

[53] Better safe than sorry.

WHY EVERYONE SHOULD CALM DOWN
AND JUST GET ON.

The thing about religions is in many ways they're like political parties, they're all pretty much the same, saying pretty much the same thing, in pretty much the same way, which basically boils down to 'behave'. Theology aside, if I have a creed at all it would be this: any religion that allows for the sale/purchase of beers etc. and pork scratchings is fine by me. And that's what I'd man the barricades for, without a shadow of a doubt. Beer and scratchings. Live and let eat scratchings I say. And of course I'm not free on Sundays because it's the busiest day for the football on Sky Sports. So in that sense I am a Christian stout and true. Just don't expect to see me in Church.

WHY FARMING IS DISGUSTING

Farming means the Countryside. I live in the city, always have always will, and I find the simple notion of the countryside disturbing. Wide open spaces, birds everywhere (I hate birds, like nasty little dead-eyed robots), animals blundering around waiting to be harvested, crapping everywhere, farmers being paid not to actually do anything and still producing too much food.

If you start to look into the whole business of farming it starts to get pretty disturbing. Take for instance the way they treat hens. All those chickens hooked up to a battery. When they want more eggs they turn up the voltage. Disgraceful ... how could you look at yourself in the mirror? And oven chips, grown in unearthly clumps of oversized yellow crystals. As for what they do if a potentially fatal disease comes along: foot and mouth, bird flu,[54] mad cow disease[55] – 'We're killing these animals so that they don't die'. Oh yeah I get it.

MILK: FOUL, UNTHINKABLE, COW-SWEAT

If you stop and think about where milk comes from, you will probably never get up and walk to the fridge again. Cows' milk comes from cows, of course it does, but what is a cow? A giant lumbering black and white monster, spattered with its own manure, piss and general filth, staggering moronically around in

[54] Have you seen a chicken sneeze? And if you have, how did you know it wasn't just allergic to feathers?
[55] Not to be confused with the Osmonds hit 'Crazy Horses'.

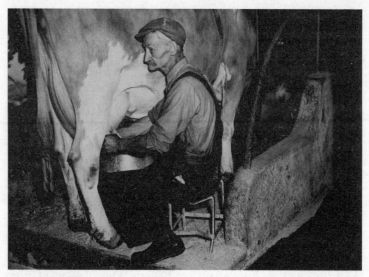
Look at the udders on that.

herds, camouflaged with its ingenious black and white colour scheme, that allows it to hide where exactly? Apart from an opencast coal mine covered in thawing snow, I mean. Amongst other cows!! That's where!! What kind of camouflage is that!?! A gigantic, filthy lumbering beast that is covered in its own excrement, urine and filth, that has to be kept at bay with electric fences and cattle prods and cattle grids, a giant lumbering idiotic beast that allows its udders, its boobs, its breasts, the very place from where the milk – on your cornflakes, in your cuppa – comes from to drag in said muck, filth, detritus. And all they have to say for themselves is moo.

Then consider what happens to said milk, or giant lumbering beastie crap-splattered boob sweat as I prefer to call it; it's sucked out of the cow with a machine that makes the cow think it's suckling a baby cow. Not that it even notices that it's a machine, that's how daft these beasts are. Then it's sent off somewhere else and pasteurised[56] so that none of the cow germs will get you (don't know what kind, but I would have thought cow pox might be amongst them, that and whatever else is normally attracted to the turd-smeared breasts of oversized idiot mammals). Still taste good? I wonder. I have no problem with eating beef on the other hand, because at least the meat lives under the skin of this monstrous thing and isn't covered in its poo. Really what I'm saying is you're far better off drinking booze, as at no stage has it leaked out of any organic life forms' bodies (at least not before you drunk it). Might as well pour it on your cereal too while you're at it.

Back Off Brussels!

Naturally the problem with farming lies largely over the water in the devil's bosom, Brussels. Amongst their many achievements in that over-paid talking shop, like... ooh, let me think now... simplifying the exchange of money abroad by forcing everyone to go over to the Euro – everyone except us, that is (over my dead body, etc.) – the utter buggering up of the farming industry. Thanks to Brussels, the once proud British farmer who had cut down all his hedgerows and made the biggest and mightiest fields the world has ever known which delivered the most food the world has ever known, has had to stop doing that, replant his hedgerows and end up having people shooting pheasants on his land at £40 a pop (and a grand day out it was too, though I think the MD at the brewery was lying about how many pheasants he shot. Seeing as I'd only ever used a shotgun to threaten on a Friday up to that point I found the whole thing a bit pointless, and

[56] French word.

I was asked to come up with a caption for this picture, but there's nothing to add.

the sight of a herd of cows had got me thinking about all the milk I'd ever drunk, and I had to be sick behind the Land Rover).

Basically what's happened is that British farmers were doing such a good job of the farming that the rest of the EEC got embarrassed. French farmers with their single onion patch, German farmers, their land ruined because of all the weapons buried at the bottom of the garden just in case (it's been too quiet, too long, if you ask me), Belgian chocolate farmers (not slang), the Dutch with their endless fields of marijuana waving in the impressionistic breeze…the others, all of them looked over here at how well we were doing and said: 'That's enough of that!'.

So Brussels cranked up the red tape machine and decreed that wildlife and hedges were more important than big bowls of cheap cornflakes; which would be fine, but have you tried roasted chaffinch? Or squirrel soup? Posh people have a word for it: 'gamey'. The other alternative is they have to rent out former farm buildings to what are these days called 'businesses' rather than firms, companies, women with a potter's wheel and buckets full of hope. So British farmers, once paid to be the mightiest farmers in the world, are now paid to administer little industrial estates where once eighteen thousand pigs were chained to a trough. Is that progress? You tell me. Having said all that wouldn't you want to shake the bloke who invented the Combine Harvester by the hand? What a brilliant invention. And then punch the bloke in the face for giving the Wurzels a hit record.

☞ THE WAY THINGS ARE

No.3: Carry On Films Are Crap

Carry On films just aren't art – you can put 'em on at film festivals as much as you like but they will not magically turn into art – leave well alone. Hands off!! They're crap, and they're not so crap they're good either, like idiots say about Hasselhoff – I'm sorry but he is just crap. Carry On films are crap, and I wouldn't have them any other way. They're making a new one, and it's going to be crap. It's the way things are.

TOP TEN CHURCHILL QUOTES:

Winston Churchill: the greatest British Britonman ever to have lived. The man who stood against the tide. The man who realised that for Britain to survive the Empire could not, but that it was a price worth paying. The man who'd got Hitler's bloody number long before anyone else. The man who went round flicking V's at the world for five years and got away with it. The man who is the reason this book isn't **auf Deutfch,**[57] and the reason this isn't your Top Ten Hitler quotes.

And the man had a way with words – when the moment arrived he had just the right thing to say, and the right way to say it. Here's a choice selection of some of the things the great man said. Read 'em, treasure 'em, learn 'em.

1) **'We shall fight them on the beaches, we will never surrender.'**
That's the stuff mate. Never surrender. Stand your ground. Hang on long enough for the Americans to figure out what's going on, and save the world. Beautiful.

2) **'You, Madam, are ugly. But in the morning, I shall be sober.'**
He said this in reply to a woman who told him he was drunk. I'd use this myself, but a) he thought of it first, b) I'm not normally sober in the morning.

3) **'Never has so much been owed by so many to so few.'**
In summing up the Battle of Britain Winston does raise the question of would we have won it quicker if there hadn't been so few pilots but manages to make it sound good and get us all off the hook.

4) **'This, was their Finest Hour.'**
Old Winston here is of course referring to Britain standing alone against Germany. And it was our Finest Hour, whether The Guardian likes it or not, no argument. Trouble is, nowadays, thanks to the telly, no one has the attention span for a Finest Hour. We'd watch about five minutes on the box and find out what was on the other side.

5) **'Always remember, I have taken more out of alcohol than alcohol has taken out of me.'**
God, I wish I could say that. Drink responsibly, kids (I have to put that in).

---

[57] In German. In German.

6) 'If you're going through Hell, keep going.'

This is an inspiring quote, though it is possible to get the wrong sense out of it. A good example of this would be when the mystery customer had popped in for a half and somehow got embroiled in a dispute over whether you should put the milk in the cup before you pour the tea, things got a bit heated, and the next thing I knew the mystery customer was there on the floor having seven shades knocked out of him. It was then that Churchill's words popped into my head – 'if you're going through Hell, keep going' – and I didn't intervene. We didn't get such a good service write up that quarter. Fight responsibly, kids.

7) 'Never give in. Never give in. Never, never, never, never.'

Alright mate, we get the point. Still, we were up to our necks in it. He'd have been hard work at breakfast wouldn't he?

The thing is there's no way that come Thursday Churchill would have been going round saying 'ooh, is it Thursday already? Where has the week gone?' That's the thing we spend our lives saying isn't it? That or 'I can't wait for the weekend' or 'I'll do it next week'. Churchill didn't think he could leave crushing Fascism till next week, he was going to do it now!! And he was never going to give in, never, never, never!!![58]

8) 'Some chicken! Some neck!'

Historians believe this to be a feisty response to Hitler's boast that he would throttle the life out of Great Britain as easily as wringing the neck of a chicken. In fact, though, I have it on good authority that old Winston had a far-off look in his eye, and was reminiscing about a Christmas dinner at Chequers in 1942, when the war was turning our way, and he'd just had a slap-up roast with all the trimmings – not just some of the trimmings, all of them – and he'd necked a pint of Old Wanger in one to win a ten bob bet with Montgomery. Happy days...

9) 'Clementine, it seems we've run out of toilet paper, but I didn't check before I sat down, be a love and grab me a roll'.

We've no real way of knowing if Churchill ever said these words, but it's a fair bet he did, he was only human, doubtless whilst waiting for news from El Alamein.

10) 'Can I have another biscuit, please'.

He definitely said that. On more than one occasion.

[58] Never.

IS MY PUB A WINE BAR?
PART 3

We now reach the acid test. No, I'm not advocating that your 'pub' should serve acid – that would be mental. No, I'm talking about the range of foodstuffs on offer.

3. SO WHAT BAR SNACKS DO THEY DO?

Let us begin with bar snacks. In a British pub, the Holy Trinity of Bar Snacks is as follows: Crisps. Nuts. Scratchings. Say it with me: Crisps, nuts, scratchings, crisps, nuts, scratchings, crisps, nuts, scratchings.

Crisps – commit to memory this handy little rhyme and you won't go far wrong: 'Ready Salted, can't be faulted, Salt 'n' Vinegar, that's a winner(gar), Cheese 'n' Onion, bags of fun(ion). Other flavours you may not savour, except Smoky Bacon, which has a waiver.'

Scratchings – pork, and I cannot stress this strongly enough, pork only. To the best of my knowledge only the pig of all God's beautiful British creatures responds edibly to being scratched. If you find you are being offered horse scratchings, or sheep, or dog, then put down your pint and leave at once. Your host has lost the plot and may be dangerous.

Nuts – the humble peanut is of course the publican's friend. Whether the traditional salted, or the once upstart but now accepted-by-all dry roasted variety, the peanut will always pull its weight, driving your punters back to the pumps.

So there we have it. Crisps, nuts, scratchings. Crisps, nuts, scratchings. Crisps, nuts, scratchings. That's what we want to see, that's what we expect to see, that is what it is our right as British citizens to see adorning our bars and stapled teasingly to cardboard photographs of page three models.

The exception that proves the rule, the very Prince of Pub Bar Snacks, is of course the unexpected jackpot: sandwiches (cheese, pickle) and sausage rolls, brought around, free and gratis, from table to table by a comely barmaid who explains, 'these are leftover from a do in the function room, seemed a shame to chuck 'em out'.

Anything else on offer in the way of bar snacks is, in my view, seriously suspect.[59]

For example:

Olives. Now, to be fair, every publican is obliged to have olives on the premises in case a customer asks for a martini, but be honest – how often is James Bond going to come in my gaff? Olives in a jar, close to if not past their sell-by-date, stuck at the back of the fridge in case of emergencies, then that's fine. Olives in a bowl, however, on the bar, or on the very tables themselves, whether black olives, green olives, or olives with red stuff in the

[59] Note: Scampi Fries, Bacon Frazzles and Cheesey Moments are technically members of the crisp family and may, under certain circumstances, be acceptable. For more information on Where Bar Snacks Come From, then see *WHERE BAR SNACKS COME FROM*.

middle – if this is what you see, then I'm sorry, your 'pub' is a wine bar. No getting round it.

Bread sticks. Wine bar. No room for appeal.

Little squares of feta cheese, drizzled with olive oil and herbs, with mini pockets of pitta bread. Sorry, mate. Wine bar.

Dips. Garlic and herb (French), tarasamasamalata (pink), salsa (a dance), and humus. Humus, I mean really. Do you remember at school, when the teacher made you all go out into the school garden and scoop up a jar of soil, and then you'd top up the jar with water, shake it up, and let it all settle down into layers? Eh? Heavy clay at the bottom, lighter sandy soil above, and then floating on the top all the bits of twigs and dead leaves and such? That, floating on the top, that's your humus, mate. You can eat it if you want, but you'll have to go to a wine bar to do it.

Nachos. The tex-mex crisp. From Tex-mexico, where scientists have perfected the triangular potato. Without dip, this is borderline acceptable, as is the kettle chip, though why they cook them in kettles is beyond me. (And how.) With dip, or as an accessory to dip – welcome to the wine bar.

If you see any of the above, then there might as well be a big red flashing neon sign out the front saying 'WINE BAR'. In fact, it's not beyond the bounds of possibility that there might be one...(you should really check for this during the pub basics, test number 1).

If you're still not sure, then see *IS MY PUB A WINE BAR PART 4.*

One or Two

How to's

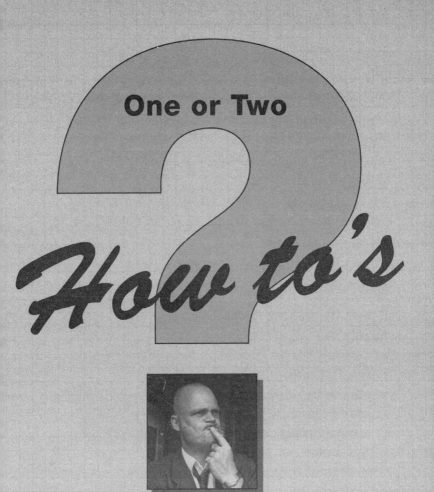

Useful Practical Advice

It was suggested to me that maybe I should include some **useful practical advice** in this compendium of Common Sense. Things that, come the moment, mean you're fully prepared to make the most of that moment. We'll start with one or two basics and work our way up to stuff you'll probably never need, though this isn't the *Worse Case* book thing, so I won't be telling you how to handle something disastrous. Besides, that's covered elsewhere.[60]

Contents:

1. PULL THE PERFECT[61] PINT
2a. TIE A TIE
2b. TIE A TIE
3. PARALLEL PARK
4. BUILD AN AIR -RAID SHELTER
5. USE THE GLASS WASHING MACHINE
6. HOOVER THE HOUSE
7. FELL A TREE
8. WHAT TO DO IF YOUR CAR FALLS INTO A RIVER

[60] See *WHAT TO DO IF YOUR CAR FALLS INTO A RIVER*.
[61] Did you know that there's no **German** word for perfect?

1. PULL THE PERFECT PINT

Step 1. It's all in the wrist and the subtle tilt of the glass. Ensure the liquid flows evenly onto the side of the glass, or else it'll bubble up and overflow – you'll get too much head on the beer. Simple really. If anything, this belongs in a Best Case Scenario Handbook.

fig. 1. Pulling Power

2a. HOW TO TIE A TIE

Step 1. Now I do like to see a gent in a tie, it denotes effort. Though not with a t-shirt, obviously. Wearing a tie denotes status, wearing a tie means you are a serious person, wearing a tie means you are smart. Though no way on earth am I doing up my top button.

fig. 1

fig. 3

fig. 2

2b. HOW TO TIE A TIE

Step 1

Step 2

Step 3

Step 1

2b. HOW TO TIE A TIE (continued)

Step 2

Step 3

Step 4

That's it love

3. PARALLEL PARK

Step 1. Well, this is something some people can't help getting wrong. And by people I mean, generalising truthfully, the ladies. It is in fact easier to parallel park than it is to go in forwards girls, because you have more manoeuvrability with the front axle. It's so easy to do I actually can't explain it. So here's a picture:

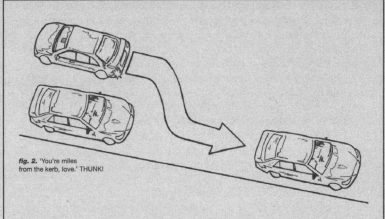

fig. 2. 'You're miles from the kerb, love.' THUNK!

Nage, involving a car.

Doubtless you will have noticed that nowhere do I make reference to doing your make up in the rear view mirror etc. Just park it. Backwards. What's wrong with you?

4. HOW TO BUILD AN AIR-RAID SHELTER
(It Could Happen, They've Been Too Quiet For Too Long)

Step 1. We survived the Blitz because of the Blitz Spirit, but also because of air raid shelters. No amount of Spirit would have rendered us immune to large amounts of German high explosive, though it would have come pretty close. Anyway, you have several options in terms of air raid shelters – though I would say that the one that fits under your dining room table might not be the one you want to go for. The one I'm talking about here is called an Anderson Shelter. We used to have one of these at the bottom of the garden at my Nan's pub, the one my brother inherited (and turned into an inexplicably successful wine bar, the bloody Judas, with his Sade records. Family, you can't choose 'em, but you can pretend they don't exist). Anyway, what you need is some corrugated iron, and it's hard to get your hands on corrugated iron these days except from disused air raid shelters, so you're pretty much robbing Peter to pay Paul here, but when it comes to building an air raid shelter you want to be the one with the corrugated iron, trust me. Go to the bottom of your garden – by the way, if you're in a flat somewhere, I'd skip this next bit – with the corrugated iron, dig an enormous hole and bend the iron into a curve and so on, you know. I've not done it myself but it should end up looking like this.

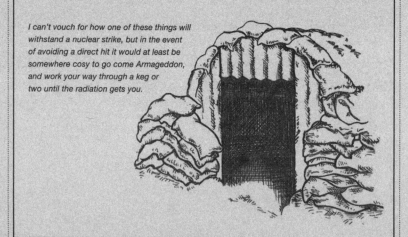

I can't vouch for how one of these things will withstand a nuclear strike, but in the event of avoiding a direct hit it would at least be somewhere cosy to go come Armageddon, and work your way through a keg or two until the radiation gets you.

5. HOW TO USE THE GLASS WASHING MACHINE

Step 1. Actually I can't help you with this one, I've lost the manual for the bloody thing. One of the girls knows how it works, which is why no matter how many bottles of Bailey's she steals I can't fire her. In fact, she's probably holding the manual hostage, even as we speak.

6. HOW TO HOOVER THE HOUSE

Step 1. Check out the Lonely Hearts ads in the local paper, try to pick one that doesn't sound too ghastly (quick tip: GSOH means ugly), grit your teeth, go on a couple of dates, buy some flowers, so on, with a bit of luck one thing will lead to another (if only I knew what that one thing was), and you can pop the question, hire a top hat for a day, and there you are, Bob's your uncle, the house is getting hoovered. I can't make any guarantees for how long such an arrangement may last; thing is you could always hire a cleaner, and when you sack her you don't have to give her half of everything. Cow.

7. HOW TO FELL A TREE

Step 1. Obvious innit? Get an axe and chop the bastard down. Don't bother with one of those helmets, let's face it, if a forty-foot tree starts to fall on you, just run round the other side. It's Common Sense. **And while we're at it, we may as well discuss:**

8. WHAT TO DO IF YOUR CAR FALLS INTO A RIVER

Step 1. Take out your copy of the book *Worst Case Scenarios*, turn to the chapter 'What to do if your car falls into a river', and read it carefully but quickly as your car sinks slowly towards the river bed, beneath the dome light, sputtering until it shorts out, with the doors buckling and the windows cracking as the water pressure rises. So anyway, good luck with that.

BIG TOPIC NUMBER TWO:
LOVE & MARRIAGE

One in three marriages end in divorce, usually your first. The second probably ends due to lack of interest, the third when the fella with the scythe steps in. My folks' ended by the last of the three, though it wasn't for want of my mum's trying to engineer the first option. My mum didn't do lack of interest, she was like nature and abhorred a vacuum. And the dusting.

Marriage: what God has brought together let no man put asunder, oh well, go on then, why not, ah, fuck it, who cares...? This is the attitude of modern times. And it's all the fault of the modern 'all the trimmings wedding'. Weddings operate very simply on the principle that you bring everyone into one place to hear the promises being made so as to embarrass you into keeping them. It's that simple. No great insight, no great moving moment, it's a simple piece of bullying, peer pressure, social welding by brute force alone. Weddings which are padded out with people you don't know, cousins you can't remember, and fat-faced friends of the bride's mum are statistically more likely (at least by my reckoning) to go under than marriages where it's just you and your mates. Cos who gives a toss what all those people you don't know think? And as you'll never see them again, so what if it turns out you didn't really mean it?

THE TWO KINDS OF WEDDING

There are two kinds of wedding: the spectator sport, and the participation event. Your own wedding will tend to fall into the latter category, though having said that a mate of mine has made a habit of getting engaged and not setting a date. He enjoys watching the whole palaver getting set up, and cashing in the commitment brownie points from having proved he is the kind of guy who is capable of popping the question, but if he doesn't ever agree a date he can let the whole thing run into the long grass…He swears by it, though he did leave one a little late, having to drop out the night before. The reception was supposed to be in my function room and I didn't give back the deposit even though I hadn't been to the Cash 'n' Carry yet to buy sandwich spread, so he wasn't the only one who felt a bit shabby about the whole incident.

Weddings can be a spectator sport, you can stand by and take it all in, enjoy the family dramatics playing themselves out in front of you, or just sink into your booze and let it all happen, drunken lunges at bridesmaids, etc., etc. All in all not a bad way of spending a Saturday when the football season's over, though you can find a wedding clashing with qualifying unless the Grand Prix is somewhere especially foreign and a few time zones away. It's my favourite spectator sport, the motor racing, as I can relate to the fact that these people are driving, and I can do that. Schumacher a genius? Nah, mate, he's just bothered practising.

As publicans we see more than our fair share of matrimonials, of every kind: husbands hiding from wives, wives retrieving hiding husbands, husbands meeting their wives, wives meeting other wives' husbands – the whole lot. Occasionally we do, in our line of business, get to participate on the catering side. For some couples having the likes of me handing out ham sandwiches and pints to their loved ones as they come out of the registry office would not be their idea of a fairytale wedding – though what fairytales have to do with weddings I don't know. Fairytales involve people getting eaten, and goblins, and they-all-lived-happily-ever-after is hardly the best way to go into getting married, surely? For other couples a pint and a pie wedding is just the dab. I'd have bloody loved it, I'm telling you...

PERSONAL EXPERIENCE IS WHAT COUNTS

When I got married it was the full blooming set piece, when honestly there would have been nothing better than sitting in the beer garden with a pint. On my own, without the newly acquired missus. Jesus, they'd gone for the lot. Does anyone and has anyone ever looked good in top hats? No, they don't. So why have they become wedding apparel – they died out with the Victorians along with Cholera[62] and having to make your own entertainment.

Another quiet afternoon in the pub.

What possible purpose does a top hat have? None can answer. Historically the top hat dates back to a time when men were much shorter. Have you ever been to the *Cutty Sark*? Christ, I had to get on my hands and knees just to get through the doorways. Men, understandably, were embarrassed about being

[62] A disease which has you crap yourself to death. Now I like a good crap as much as the next man, but that is no way to go now is it?

such shortarses, and thought that sticking a stovepipe on top of their heads would give them the stature they craved. It's a pretty transparent ruse, though, and it's had its day. You wouldn't catch Hollywood tinyman Tom Cruise in a top hat, and he'll do anything to add a couple of illusory inches. Nowadays it's all done with platform shoes and getting your co-star to stand in a hole. Imagine Tom Cruise with platform shoes AND a top hat, though. He'd be a giant amongst men. Trouble is, it's such a difficult look to carry off, unless you're Noddy Holder.

Dammit, I'm still angry about the money I pissed away on that hat. Though of course it wasn't my money, it was my father-in-law's money, but it was still pissed away, that's my point. If only I could have made him understand that a pint and a ploughman's in a beer garden with nothing but the sound of the flyover and the planes stacking on their way into Heathrow would have been preferable. Oh for a quiet life.

MOTHER-IN-LAW JOKES

The transmogrification[63] of your bird's mum into a mother-in-law is a terrifying thing, and no less terrifying even though now we don't tell mother-in-law jokes any more do we?? Those jokes were born not of necessity but of grim, desperate reality.

Mother-in-law jokes are out of fashion these days, though I don't really know why.[64] It wasn't like they hurt anyone – they were about a mythical mother-in-law, not about someone real in any way; a totemistic version of the mother-in-law, like a giant or

[63] There's a proper £80 word.
[64] Perhaps this is why marriage is in such tragic decline, people are desperate to avoid making mother-in-law jokes. Don't ask me, I'm not a sociologist.

142

dragon – they weren't meant to be anything to do with the reality of things. Those jokes of course came from a time when your family all lived in the one house, not scattered all across the place in various flats. Living like that on top of each other would be bound to cause trouble, especially given the future echo that every mother-in-law represents: one look at her tells you that this is what your missus is going to be like and it's *only a matter of time*. So forgive our forefathers for making such jokes when the opportunity arose, they were only laughing in the face of fear, which was probably the only defence mechanism left to them.

And there was plenty to fear from my mother-in-law. She had squeezed herself into a classic mutton-accentuating outfit – everything about what she wore pointed away from the idea that she was lamb. Her calves, taut with the strain of the heels she was wearing, didn't so much totter as oscillate: science could never explain how she'd get around. The skirt of her suit was cut just above the knee, and you could tell from her glistening piggy eyes and leaden flirting that this was something she was pleased about in

They'll never replace the old stars will they? Though Johnny Vegas isn't far off if we're honest.

the extreme. The push-up bra was doing its evil work, complicit like a German railway worker in 1944. She thought she looked fantastic and prowled around flirting with my mates in a way that was simultaneously ridiculous and threatening. You didn't know where to look, and you couldn't look anywhere else.

THE VICAR

Vicars. A dying breed. Bless. They're up there spouting this crap, and they know – especially at a wedding – that they're on the meter and that no one, least of all the happy couple, are listening. How do they do it? How does he get up in the morning, put on the frock and march out into the world of old ladies, cups of tea, ignorant hand wringing – ask not for who the hands wring, vicar, they wring for you. All the old ladies now care about is whether their vicar's gay or not. And whether he's going to Hell, which they aren't. Nightmare.

So there's the vicar and he's got this 'I don't believe any of this stuff either' expression on, and his eyes are moving independently of one another, and you can tell that if you got six drinks into him his eyes would straighten and he'd spill his guts and tell you that the Bible's all bollocks, that obviously Jesus didn't come back from the dead, and really, all he wanted to do was help people and maybe go into medicine but he was too thick to become a doctor, too timid to become a nurse and too weak to become a hospital porter.

Why marriage has anything to do with the Church these days is a greater mystery than the Virgin Birth (which I think folks shouldn't worry about

– if God can knock up the world in seven days then he can knock up a virgin, easy, no trouble, see *RELIGION*). Getting married in church for modern normal people is like going sailing in the age of the outboard motor: get over it, it's unnecessary fuss, it's a waste of time and effort, get over it. And what you and Doris getting married has to do with God who is busy faminising or pestilencing whoever he's decided to smite this time, beats me. He surely has bigger fish to fry than you and the missus to be. Surely.

CONCLUSIONS? YOU'LL BE LUCKY

So it becomes clear that the average wedding – and you will forgive me if I now blunder into the obvious observation – serves one purpose and one purpose only: it gives the mother-in-law something to do, that's all. And, if you do the right thing and hand it all over to her, then she'll actually create the perfect recipe for a marriage destined to go belly up. She invites all her pals who you don't know and who she says flirty things to you in front of, and hey presto! She's created the wedding you can't possibly care less about, the wedding without peer pressure, the wedding that frankly doesn't particularly count…and then they stick a top hat on you, it's as good as having your fingers crossed behind your back whilst making your vows.

THE FOREIGN LEGION

Many drinkers are, of course, drinking to forget, but the other option for those wanting to forget is the French Foreign Legion. And though Laurel and Hardy may have joined the French Foreign Legion[65] it is something I myself would not consider because:

a)   it's French

b)   it's Foreign

c)   it clearly requires more effort than raising a pint to your lips. I'm not running round in the desert with a back-pack full of rocks for anyone, let alone Jacques Chirac or whoever.

The first time I died in a pub fire[66] I did think quite seriously about joining, but the feeling wore off quite quickly. The second and third times it didn't even occur to me. I did try to join the British Legion, but it's not quite the same thing, and I have enough old soldiers drinking in my gaff – I feel I'm doing more use than I ever would shaking a charity tin outside Woolies. Plus the uniform isn't that good: it's a cagoule.

[65] Mind you, it was for comedy purposes.
[66] For insurances purposes, keep up.

The thick one was British.
That's why they were funny.

ISAAC NEWTON (1643-1727)
English scientist and thinker, said

'Behold, I have discovered gravity.'

You reckon? Calm down, Isaac, you haven't discovered gravity. Everyone knows all about it already. You don't see us all floating off into space, do you? You named gravity, that's what you did. You gave it the name 'gravity'. Well done. What you discovered, in point of fact, was that sitting under an apple tree in the autumn is not the brightest place to do your thinking. Having said that, though, if you are going to sit there then you could do a lot worse than one of those wigs Isaac used to wear. I imagine they'd absorb a fair bit of apple impact, like a seventeenth- century crash helmet.

No, the best place for thinking is in the bog while flicking through AutoTrader, where the only thing that could possibly fall on your head is a loose cistern when the bolts have rusted through, and that's only happened twice in the whole time I've been a landlord, and only one of those times was actually fatal.

BEAUTIFUL BRITISH
FOLK TALES

Make no mistake about it – Greek mythology is fantastic. Look at Ulysses. Some blokes can get away with anything can't they? He buggers off for ten years, and when he gets back his wife says, 'Here's your dinner, my hero!' None of that, 'What time do you call this?' business. None of that, 'You've been out with the boys again, haven't you?' Good old Ulysses mutters something vague about a decade-long war and tucks into the kebab and oven chips. Inspiring stuff.

And what do we learn from the tale of Perseus and the Medusa? Well, it's all Common Sense. If you look at an ugly bird you'll get turned to stone. We all know that feeling, don't we? But if old Perseus had been experiencing a drought like the one I'm currently staggering through he might have slung down a couple of pints of snakebite and risked it. I mean, how bad could it be?

Then of course there's the myth of Oedipus, who killed his dad and married his mother. Now I don't know about you but if I'd done that I wouldn't have told anyone, I'd have kept it to myself, I certainly wouldn't have hoped it was still a legend three thousand years later. Urgh. And to think they locked up our plane spotters. And to think the Greeks think that they're normal.

But they do have the most amazing stories. Jason and the Argonauts, all that bother because he couldn't find his fleece.

Take a bomber jacket, Jason, it's the Med, how cold is it going to get?

The Trojan Wars all that lot, tales of heroics, ingenuity, exploration and endeavour, all set in a bloody war which started because the Trojan prince Paris – French, by the sound of him – abducted the Greek queen Helen. And that Wooden Horse – that must have taken some feeding, eh? And how did they train it which soldiers to stamp on and which ones to leave alone? Genius.

It's the stuff Charlton Heston was put on this earth to star in.

Robin Hood

Now then. Although the Greek stuff is fantastic, for my money the best folk tales in the world, pound for pound, are the British folk tales. And the best folk hero in the world, bar none, is Mr Robin Hood.

A true British hero...

In the olden days there were two sorts of people living in this great land of ours. The Saxons, who were British, and therefore Good. And the Normans, who were French, and therefore Bad. Good King Richard the Lionheart, who was British, went off to the Crusades,[67] and left his brother Bad Prince John, who was French, in charge. Now even though they

[67] See *THE CRUSADES – CLUB 1130*.

were brothers, one was British and the other one was French. You work it out – that's Royal Families for you. At least one of the Princes wasn't ginger.

...lest we forget.

So Robin Hood comes back early from the Crusades and finds the Normans in charge. They've nicked his house and his girlfriend, and he has to go and live in the forest even though he's posh, but he's happy to do it because the British aristocracy are happy to muck in. Look at the Queen Mum during the Blitz.

Robin decides he'll steal from the rich Normans and give to the poor Saxons, keeping only a small proportion for his own overheads and occasional blowouts with his team, who are hence known as The Merry Men. These include an enormous bloke called Little John, which is what passed for humour in them olden days, a lad called Will Scarlet about whom the fewer questions asked the better, and a fat super-monk whose special power was eating everything within reach called Friar Tuck (the clue's in the name).

The Sheriff of Nottingham (French) and his evil sidekick Sir Guy of Gisborne (also French) tried all sorts of tricks to catch Robin, but he was always too clever for them. They knew he was the best archer in the world, so they had an archery contest, which some other geezer was winning, but then Robin's arrow splits the other bloke's arrow in half so he's the winner after all, but oh no!

The Sheriff has him cornered now, and says something like: 'Ha ha! Now I have you, Hood!' But Robin cuts a rope or something and swishes up into the chandelier and then sneaks out of a window and jumps down onto a horse and they get out under the portcullis just in time etc., etc., etc. and back to Sherwood Forest.

He loved King and Country, he hated the French, he had a little moustache, and at times of great peril, he put his hands on his hips and laughed. Ha ha ha! And everyone wore tights in them days, not just him, so there was nothing strange about him. Not like that Will Scarlet. And he was British through and through.

If the Greeks had Charlton Heston, we had Errol Flynn.

The Rest

If Robin is the best, what about the rest? There was **Dick Turpin**, of course, the dandy highwayman. Very similar to Robin Hood, except where Robin Hood stole from the rich and gave to the poor, Dick Turpin stole from everybody and kept it for himself. Legend has it he once rode his horse, Black Bess (stolen), from London to York in fifteen hours, which sounds like bollocks to me. He'd have had to go up the A1 and the Eddie Stobarts would have just put the wind up a horse, I reckon. And anyway it's snarled up around Sandy, always has been. He'd have been lucky to

An eighteenth-century hoodie on horseback.

do it in a week. The telling point here is that Dick Turpin was neither Charlton Heston nor Errol Flynn. He was Richard O'Sullivan, out of *Man About the House*.

The Romans had Romulus and Remus, the twin brothers who founded their city. In this tale the boys are suckled by a she-wolf, and...ugh...milk is bad enough, but wolf milk? Weird, the Romans.

The Spanish have El Cid, don't they. And what does their greatest folk hero of all do on the night before the great battle he must win to save his people? He dies, that's what. How heroic is that? He gets a great big bloody spear stuck right through him and dies: so much for mañana.[68] Typical of the Spanish to have a folk hero like that. I mean, what can you expect when half of the crowd at a bullfight are supporting the bull? Eh? Still, at least he was Charlton Heston in the film, which is a point in his favour, even if he is dead.

Then there was William Tell, a time waster from Switzerland. While Robin Hood was firing arrows at the Sheriff's men, the Normans, and winning archery contests, what was William Tell doing, eh? Shooting at fruit. Bloody circus act. That tells you all you need to know about the Swiss, in my view. They were lucky he shot that apple. He could have taken a fruit peeler attachment out of his Swiss army knife, peeled it, and cut it into segments for the assembled company. What a story that would have made.

[68] Spanish word. I'll tell you what it means tomorrow.

152

FRANCIS BACON (1561-1626),
English philosopher, statesman, essayist and
inventor of empirical science, said:

'Knowledge is power'

Oh please, you doughnut. I know Francis lived back in the Elizabe-
than times but he couldn't have got that one more wrong. Knowledge isn't power, electricity is power! You can't plug a hoover into an
encyclopaedia can you ladies? No! Dear oh dear what a time waster.

IS MY PUB A WINE BAR?
PART 4

If the bar snackage checks out OK, then we can move on to question 4. If of course there were breadsticks and feta cheese bites in evidence then you have probably already left the establishment in question and further testing is redundant.

CAN I HAVE A LOOK AT THE MENU, PLEASE?

Beware of cartoon pictures of food setting up unreasonable expectations.

Now ideally, of course, your 'pub' will have a carvery, which is the Rolls Royce of pub catering. The aim being to provide Sunday lunch, with all the trimmings, every day of the week all year round including Sundays.

A word on trimmings. Don't stint on the trimmings. People invariably want all of them. You will never hear someone come up to your carvery and say, 'I'd like the roast beef please, with some of the trimmings – not all, just some.' Or, 'Hey! Easy on the trimmings there, mate!' People want what's coming to them, so remember: always provide all the trimmings. *All* of them.

Not all pubs will have a carvery, and there's no shame in that, apart from the shame of not having a carvery. Where there's a kitchen, and a work experience youth in a hairnet, you can still find:

Beautiful British Pub Grub

SERVED ALL DAY – EVERYDAY

Pie	1.25	Pie Pie Beans	3.75
Chips	1.00	Pie Chips Chips	4.00
Beans	.75	Pie Beans Beans	4.25
Pie Chips	2.25	Beans Beans Chips	2.50
Pie Beans	2.00	Beans Beans Pie	2.75
Pie Beans Chips	3.25	Chips Chips Pie	3.25
Pie Chips Beans	3.50	Chips Chips Beans	2.75
Chips Beans Pie	3.75	Pie Pie Pie	3.75
Chips Pie Beans	4.00	Beans Beans Beans	2.25
Beans Pie Chips	4.25	Chips Chips Chips	3.00
Beans Chips Pie	4.50	Ploughmans[69]	5.00
Pie Pie Chips	3.50	Extra Pie, Chips, Beans add	.50

So check out the menu. Ask yourself this: is it laminated? Is it in a little spongy folder with the 'pub''s name embossed on the front? Is there a little blackboard showing 'Todays' Specail', which

[69] For centuries your British ploughman has got up in the morning, had his ploughman's breakfast, then gone out into the field, ploughed away all morning, up and down, backwards and forwards, ploughing away, turning the British sod, until he looks up, takes a big red spotted hanky from his corduroy trousers to mop his ruddy brow, sees the sun is at its zenith, and thinks to himself: 'You know what I fancy now? A slab of British cheese, with a bit of lettuce, a tomato, and a dollop of pickle, a hunk of crusty bread and butter, and a pint of British ale. I'm off to the pub.' Well, bad news, mate. Your pub has been taken over by a couple of graduates from a catering college near Ipswich, and you're having falafel. Mediterranean countries don't have the Ploughman's Lunch, that is a fact, and there's two main reasons for this. One: the ground tends to be much harder and very hilly, so they cut it into steps to make it easier to irrigate, which makes it virtually impossible to plough. Two: they're all asleep at lunchtime.

turns out on closer inspection to be something that is already available on the regular menu? Then all may be well. You may be in a Beautiful British Pub.

BUT...

Is the menu written up on a gigantic blackboard which covers most of one wall?

Are the items, upon closer inspection, not written up in chalk, but artfully painted on to look like chalk handwriting?

Do you see the phrase 'Thai fish cakes', or shepherds pie with a mash made from either sweet potatoes or butternut squash, or the words 'cracked black pepper'?

Are the dishes described at great and unnecessary lengths, including how they were cooked, i.e. 'pan-fried' (how the hell else are you going to bloody fry something...?).

Is the cutlery properly available in a self-service rack next to the condiments, or perhaps wrapped in napkins and stuffed into a pint glass, OR...are there tables laid ready for dining? With table mats showing scenes from Welsh railway journeys? And if you sit there just to have a pint and not to eat anything, citing the 'beer is food' principle, are you frowned upon, tutted at, and even asked to leave?

If all this is ringing an alarm bell for you, then, my friend, your 'pub' is not a wine bar. It is not even a wine bar masquerading as a pub. It is something far far worse. Your pub has become... gah!...A GASTRO-PUB.

Now then. I may be biased in my assessment of this phenomenon, owing to an incident some time back when I lost a tooth taking a bite out of a meat pie that was in fact made of pottery with a pastry lid, but, in my view, gastro- belongs exclusively with -enteritis and not with -pub.

There is, I must admit, a lot of pressure on today's publican to 'go gastro', especially from the breweries. My brewery were very keen on sushi a while back. Sushi, of course, is the Japanese word for 'I can't be bothered to cook this'. Anyway, it was fashionable, and they were wanting us to attract a more yuppie clientele, for reasons best known to themselves but probably involving shifting more **German** beer where the mark up is something shocking. (Japanese food, **German** beer, I ask you. It would have been worse if they'd won, I keep telling myself, but how much worse could it get...?) So, anything for a quiet life, I tried offering sushi chicken and chips for a bit, but frankly it was a disaster. Never seen such a queue for the bogs – people were just giving up and puking in the car park – and hardly anyone could manage even one raw chip, let alone a whole potato wedge.

Would the brewery be told, though? Course not. Before we knew what was what, they'd delivered a whole batch of raw fish, with instructions how to roll it up and stick a cocktail stick in it. Well, I knew we'd never get rid of the stuff, but then British thinking came to the rescue. I got Anthony, the seventeen-year-old work experience youth, to deep fry the lot in batter and we sold it in baskets with chips.

The trouble with going gastro is the necessity of dealing with a chef. Chef is of course a French word, meaning 'cook with ideas above his station'. No self-respecting landlord will allow a chef on his premises if he knows what's good for him. Otherwise before he knows it he'll be hearing things like: 'Thees is my keetchen!' and 'I do not do cheeps! I cook French Fried potatoes to a Belgian recipe!'

I'll just say this. A pub divided against itself cannot stand, and a landlord must be master of all he surveys. Besides which, there's a never-ending supply of work experience lads to boss around, who are all perfectly capable of taking a beautiful British lasagne out of the freezer, bunging it in the beautiful British microwave, and then whacking it into a beautiful British basket with some chips.

I hope this has been helpful.

If you're still not sure, then see *IS MY PUB A WINE BAR PART 5*.

WIND TURBINES – IT'S ONLY A BLOODY WINDMILL

It was William Blake, I think (dunno, might not have been, I don't care) who sang about the dark satanic mills that plunder the landscape of Britain in his patriotic song 'Jerusalem'. And you know what? Nothing's changed has it – now you've got all these miserable bastards banging on about wind turbines.

They want to have their cake and eat it, you can't spend hundreds of years rinsing electricity with your electric toothbrushes and the like, and not expect to make some sacrifice. And some poncy pastoral view isn't much of a sacrifice is it, especially when there's no one living there?

Yes I'm talking to you, sitting there well into the night, cock in hand at your computer or lying on the sofa spending all day ironically watching back-to-back re-runs of *The A-Team* on Bravo. Grow up. What do you want, eh? You've already made half of Wales unemployed by using up all the coal and then you turn into Bono on a Greenpeace march when the word 'Nuclear' is even mentioned. It's called progress! You all want to see it; you just don't want to actually be able to see it.

Wind turbines aren't that bad are they? They're like modern windmills; and the reason for this is in fact that's exactly what they are: windmills. Get over it. But oh no, you don't like those do you, you're quite happy with the great big dirty pylons bringing

159

you the electricity but not the mills making it. You haven't thought it through have you? So what is the alternative?

HERE'S THE ALTERNATIVE...

We erect a series of large hamster wheels all along the South Downs, we have thousands of hamsters that are fed steroids to keep them running through the night, these are linked up to generators that create the energy that powers the nation. Job done, can we go home? But hang on, who's this on the horizon? Marvellous, it's the Animal Rights nutters. And we are not talking your Swampy-style pacifists. We are talking the weapon-wielding variety. However, the police are too busy doing the paperwork for speeding fines and the people who haven't bought bus tickets to deal with these Vegan vigilantes, so the Army are called in. After a few casualties and one tear gas-related fatality, they come to the agreement that the only solution is to swap the hamsters for a load of children. They are eager, keen and have lots of energy.

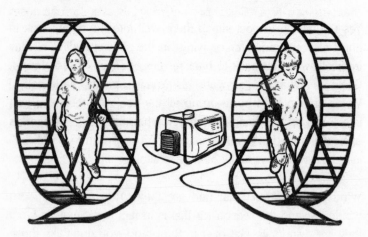

I've thought it through for you, and you don't like it.

Job done, now can we go home? Please tell me it's not, it is! It's the weirdos from Amnesty International, bloody do-gooders. Apparently we've violated some la-di-da human rights law and the kids are not supposed to be running constantly for 24 hours straight.

Then, over the hill come the fat women in shell suits from the nearest estate who are shouting because they heard it was something to do with child abuse and have come with their kids and some placards made out of cereal boxes with bad spelling on. Of course, their children have no idea what's going on.

Then it kicks off between the Animal Rights and the Army because they still haven't got over the use of dogs in WWII. So the UN come steaming in as by now it's really got out of hand.

The Americans get word the UN are involved and think it's something to do with them so they get stuck in. You can't blame them though; it's a reflex action and the global version of a nosey neighbour.

And to top it all off one of the kids on the hamster wheel has sneaked in a mobile phone and has called Childline. Next thing you know Esther Rantzen turns up and is screaming bloody murder. Well done you've just started WWIII and over what? A windmill. This isn't Holland, get over it.

THE ZULU DRINKING GAME

Zulu is of course the film we've all watched countless times on a Sunday afternoon and wondered if they would get away with making such a thing these days. Basically a load of historically inaccurate Welshmen, led by a John Cleese lookalike and Michael Caine playing a posh bloke, are attacked by thousands of Zulus wearing leg-warmers and/or Womble boots, and it gets very very nasty especially if you're trying to teach race relations.

To play this game you will need:

1 X VIDEO OF *ZULU*, AND LOADS OF BEER PER PERSON.[70]

First things first, fast forward the tape an hour a) because it really does go on a bit for the first bit and b) because it looks funny in fast forward. Seriously, nothing much happens during this first bit apart from lots of people explaining what's going on and Michael Caine talking in a strange strangled accent that normally would end every sentence with the word 'ducky'. There's a noteworthy scene at the start involving hundreds of semi-naked bosomy ladies dancing that somehow gets shown on Sunday afternoons without comment that you may want to stop and peruse.

[70] Please watch Zulu responsibly.

162

Things only really hot up after the cowboys, who are plainly on the wrong part of the 20th Century Fox film lot and on their way back to catering for lunch, say they're not going to stick around and fight the Zulus. Then the Zulus turn up and it's time to get your drinks to the ready.

What you want to do is take sides – you can drink for the Welsh or for the Zulus. The main rule is you take a drink each time one of the 'enemy' dies, or take a drink when one of your own side is killed. So if you're on the side of the Welsh you're going to need to be able to put it away given how many Zulus bite the dust, but then the Welsh are great drinkers so you don't want to let the side down do you? When the Welsh drink they have to shout 'Yaki da!' (is that how it's spelt? You know I'm not going to get round to checking) and when the Zulus drink they have to shout 'Zulu!'

OTHER TIMES TO DRINK ARE:

 When the missionary, played by Jack Hawkins, rides off into nowhere screaming 'you're all going to die!'. Both sides drain your glass.

 The obligatory 'Why Scene' from all sixties war films, when someone asks 'Why? Why?' over and over to excuse the fact that actually this is a war film and has no point at all. Both sides drink and take time to ponder why.

 Drink whenever the action cuts to the film set in Twickenham and we are plainly no longer on the South African veldt.

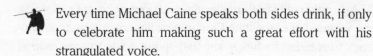

Every time Michael Caine speaks both sides drink, if only to celebrate him making such a great effort with his strangulated voice.

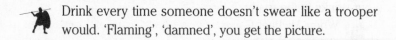

Drink every time someone doesn't swear like a trooper would. 'Flaming', 'damned', you get the picture.

When there's some gratuitous Welshery, Welshness or Welsh-itude. No shortage of this – it can be Welsh blokes singing Welshly, Welsh blokes cursing English people for no reason other than that they're English, or simply looking miserable because they're not in Wales, or just because they're Welsh.

Hook (nickname 'Hooky', God bless the British Army) goes to extraordinary lengths to get at the brandy in the medical cupboard, bless him – when he finally does, drain your glass.

When the cattle are released pointlessly (though it may be to make the film resemble a Western and therefore more comprehensible to Americans) many Zulus die. Seeing as these Zulus are dying by cattle, both sides take a drink for each Zulu killed.

Towards the end of the movie they all start talking about how thirsty they are. Have a drink. You can.

If you're on the Zulus' side sing near the end when the Zulus sing. Sing whatever you like, they seem to be. Take a drink.

164

When the Welsh sing near the end by all means join in, but you have to drink: 'Welshmen never yield!'. To be honest for all they know the Zulus are shouting 'you'rrrrrrrrrrrrrrrree shit! Ah!' in Zulu.

 When Michael Caine says he feels ashamed drain your glass, if only because he's right.

 Have a drink at any point that you might have said 'Oh Christ!'

 Both sides have a drink each time a VC nomination is read out. It's all about valour.

The winner, not unlike the film, will be the last one standing amongst the revolting deluge of twitching casualties.

COACH MANAGER PUNDIT PUB – WHY FOOTBALL IS NOT AS GOOD AS IT USED TO BE.

Football is not as good as it used to be. That's a fact. It's Common Sense.

The thing is, you see, what it all comes down to, is this: footballers get paid far too much money.

I'm not jealous, don't get me wrong. I'm not jealous that some seventeen-year-old Herbert who's never lived but who happens to have a freakish ability to bounce a pig's bladder on his head gets paid more in a week than I've seen in the last eight tax years. Although, actually, I don't have tax years on account of being dead for Revenue purposes.

No, the problem I have is that it has disrupted the natural order of things. Once upon a time, you see, a footballer would start winding down towards the end of his career, his knees and ankles all clogged up with cortisone residue, and there'd be four distinct and traditional options open to him. And they are as follows: Coach, Manager, Pundit and Pub.

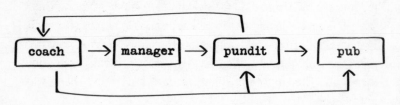

He could turn to coaching, saying something like: 'Football has been my life and I want to give something back.' (i.e. 'I don't know anything else about anything, but I've seen another bloke putting some cones out on the pitch and I reckon I could do that'.)

If he was any good at sums, he could maybe give managing a go. There's a lot of paperwork, though, for your ex-footballer to deal with, and it can be tricky trying to work out exactly what percentage of a big transfer deal should be paid directly to him in a brown paper bag at a motorway service station.

There's punditry, which could range from sitting next to Jimmy Hill on Match of the Day all the way down to covering reserve games for local radio. Generally this line of work is open to ex-footballers who are quite well-known, have actually achieved something, and aren't repulsive to look at, so it's not for everyone.

And then there was running a pub, providing he hadn't already pissed away his nest egg imagining he'd be able to play football for ever.

Those were the four options, and everybody knew where they stood. The occasional loner tried to break the mould. Ray Wilson, for example, one of the Boys of '66, went into undertaking, which is a bit of a leap, but it must have been a great comfort to a great many people over the years to see their loved ones popped into the furnace by a bona fide national hero. Essentially, though, that was it. You could go coach, then pub. You could go coach, manager, pub. You could go manager, pundit, pub. You could go pundit, coach, pundit again, manager, coach, pundit again, and then pub. The important thing, though, was pub. There was always pub.

The tradition of the ex-footballer turned publican is an ancient and noble one. Back in 1890, the Athletic Journal had this to say:

'A footballer behind the bar is as great an attraction as a long-legged giant or a fat woman.'

Imagine if Peter Crouch bought a pub – double bubble! Dawn French goes halves with him – they'd have themselves a bona fide super pub!

Alf Common, famously the first footballer to be transferred for £1000 when he moved from Sunderland to Middlesbrough back in 1905, was a jolly, red-faced, rather tubby player, famous for his attempts to lose weight. At the age of 30 Alf was transferred to Woolwich Arsenal, who devised all sorts of physical exercises and strenuous walks to get him to slim down, without success, but in the end they gave up and bowed to the inevitable. In his mind the 5'8", 13 stone Alf was already a publican, and sure enough he shortly (and fatly) left to run the Alma Hotel at Cockerton.

Fergie. Before he was the Gaffer, he was a Guv'nor.

Sir Alex Ferguson, arguably the greatest manager football has ever seen, didn't go straight to manager. He didn't even go coach manager. He couldn't, in fact, go pundit because he looked like the back of a bus and no one could understand a word he said. No, his first thought when his playing career with Rangers and Ayr United was coming to an end was, yes, you've guessed it, to get himself a pub. He didn't get that red face from running around outdoors, oh no. And if it's good enough for Fergie…

Geoff Hurst banged in those three goals for England and you'd reckon he'd be set up for life, wouldn't you, but no, he still had a crust to make. He had a go at coach, had a go at being manager at Chelsea, he's done his fair share of pundit work (on Anglia), he even tried to market a range of green football boots (how would that work? How would you see the players' feet? How would you see your own feet? He didn't think

At this point he had never pulled a pint in his life.

it through) but along the way he also bought a pub. The Sheet Anchor in Baldwin's Gate near Stoke – you can't go wrong with a nautical theme, even when you're 80 miles from the sea. Classic – nets, barrels, portholes, can't argue with that. And thus he covered all the ex-footballer bases. That belated knighthood more than deserved, I'd say.

Terry Neill was manager of Hull City, Northern Ireland, Arsenal and Spurs, but when he finally accepted that it wasn't working out for him what did he do? Opened a pub (technically a Sports Bar, but we'll let him off).

And what about **Gordon Ramsay**, eh? Used to kick a ball about for Glasgow Rangers, and what's he doing now? I suppose he'd have something to say about it, but you could argue that what he's done is he's gone into the pub trade. A glorified pub, a pub with ideas *way* above its station, no doubt about it, but at heart he's a footballer-turned-publican.

CONCLUSION

Footballers nowadays, though, they don't know they're born. Couple of years in Chelsea reserves and they never have to work again. Look at Schmeichel, look at Lee Sharpe. *Strictly Come Dancing? Love Island? Dancing on Ice?* That's not punditry, mate, that's just poncing about. These people don't need the dosh – they've already got the sort of loot set aside that you only really need if you're an evil genius planning to put together a sinister organisation to take over the world. And where's it all come from? The satellite television subscriptions of the nation's publicans, that's where.

Who are the losers on football's crazy cock-eyed money-go-round? Well we are, we all are, you and me, but most especially the pub trade. We've lost a whole generation of would-be – *should-be* – publicans, and we're never getting them back.

And that's why football's not as good as it used to be.

JEAN PAUL SARTRE (1905-1980)
French philosopher and writer, said

'Hell is other people'

Oh yeah? Fact is, Jean Paul Sartre here has made a cardinal error. Thing is, he was French, so his only experience of other people was French people, so little wonder he arrived at this conclusion. If he had simply got out more and visited, say, Britain, he might have discovered that Hell isn't other people, but is in fact France. Think it through Jean Paul, get a little perspective mate. If he'd said 'Hell is French People' he would have caused little argument. Jean Paul also went on about how the universe is a figment of your own imagination, but that's bollocks because if I had imagined the universe I would have imagined it without France in it – and therefore not old JPS himself, the whingeing git. Think it through! And let's not forget that the French word for think is ponce.

TELEVISION – A BRITISH INVENTION

Firstly what I will say is that it's a remarkable bit of British thinking,[71] putting two things together like that: 'Tele', meaning noise, and 'vision' meaning pictures. Genius. I don't see the attraction myself but I'm not going to knock it. It's just that I've got better things to do. You've got to remember I work in the evenings, so while you lot are sitting on your arses, I'm earning an honest crust.[72]

TV was invented by John Logie Bear, a Scottish bloke that was too tight to spend his evenings down the pub. (Thanks a lot for that mate, I'd be a bloody millionaire by now if you hadn't given them something else to do other than drink.) He came up with something that he could look at, but didn't expect him to engage in a conversation, the minute he got back from a long day's graft. He also managed to fit a switch that meant he could turn the thing off when either he disagreed with what it was saying, or, he felt his eyes going while it droned on late into the night. Plus, it played you the *National Anthem* to wake you up and remind you to get to bed because you had work in the morning to earn money and pay tax[73] to keep the Queen Mother in Gin and cigarettes. God bless this country.

[71] See *BRITISH THINKING*.
[72] It would be honest if I paid tax, but as I've mentioned I've died three times for this very reason.
[73] See above.

Of course he didn't know what the state of affairs would be some eighty years later, otherwise I think he may have thought twice about being so quick to wheel the thing out of his garage. It's hard to imagine what it must have been like when people first saw it, it must have seemed like a kind of magic (see *QUEEN*). In a

In the old days the whole family watched TV together, even when there was nothing on.

way it's lucky that Mrs Logie Bear didn't think of it, as in those days she would have been burnt at the stake for being a witch. The other way of course meant she would have been plunged into a river and been given the option of either,

1)   Holding her breath and surviving only to be deemed a witch and killed or,

2)   Taking her fate on the chin and drowning straight off.

No, he was pretty pleased with himself at the time, old Logie Bear. If only he'd realised that actually what he'd invented was a way for us all to watch Changing Rooms. That would have wiped the smile off his face.

The thing is that people say kids grow up fast these days, but who is it saying this? It's adults that sit in watching Doctor Who (which we have already established is For Kids). So what does this all mean? I'll tell you what it means, it means the world has gone bloody mad, all the adults are in watching kids' TV and the kids are all out getting pissed, fat and pregnant!

IS MY PUB A WINE BAR?
PART 5

Hopefully your mind is now at rest, now that you have worked your way through my checklist. Either you can now say with some confidence that your 'pub' is a proper pub, and you can drink away to your heart's content without fearing the lash of society's scorn, or you know for certain the horrible truth – your 'pub' is really a wine bar – or *worse*, it's a...gah!...*gastro* pub. Vine leaves, that's another thing to watch out for, things wrapped in vine leaves. And mozzarella cheese. And beware the aubergine.

A word of warning, though. You might want to take a quick squint at this last section, just to be on the safe side.

OTHER THINGS TO WATCH OUT FOR.

Does your 'pub' have any or all of the following?

High wing-backed leather seating to conceal snoozing.

Drinks delivered on a silver tray by 90-year-old waiters at death's door.

No women, not even working behind the bar or cleaning up sick in the toilets.

Copies of *The Times* wedged inside large wooden sticks.

A large fireplace with a chiming clock on the mantelpiece, where a man in tails and a high collar is declaiming: 'I declare that I, Phileas Fogg, shall travel around the world in no more than eighty days!'

If you have answered YES, then your 'pub' is in fact a Victorian gentleman's club.

Does your 'pub' have any or all of the following?

A name like Kickers, or Booters, or Batters.

Twelve gigantic television screens all showing Japanese baseball even though there is an England game on.

Exclusively American bottled beers, and no glasses (saves washing up, though, I suppose).

Football shirts inexplicably framed behind glass and stuck up on the wall, as if there might one day be some kind of emergency that can only be sorted out by a footballer breaking the glass and putting the shirt on.

If you have answered YES, then your 'pub' is in fact a sports bar.

Does your 'pub' have any or all of the following?

A wide range of beers, wines and spirits, with tempting discounts for bulk purchasing.

A ripe and bearded clientele which strongly favours ciders and Special Brew.

Optional brown paper bag drinks holders.

Outdoor seating, maybe on a wall or a doorstep, with an uncluttered view of the main road.

Small children hovering around the entrance begging you to buy them fags.

Alfresco toilet facilities in the doorway of Dixons.

If you have answered YES, then your 'pub' is in fact an off licence.

Does your 'pub' have any or all of the following?

A queueing system, coordinated by a pre-recorded woman's voice directing you to 'Cashier number five' or similar (number may vary).

Television screens showing nothing but adverts for house insurance even though there is an England game on.

No seating at all, but some limited facility for bar leaning.

Barmaid has a big rack, full of blank forms for vehicle licensing and temporary passports.

Alfresco toilet facilities in the doorway of Dixons.

If you have answered YES, then your 'pub' is in fact a post office.

With any luck this will have removed all possible areas of confusion, so raise a glass of beautiful British ale and drink to the beautiful British pub, and hope to God that you're actually standing in one. Cheers!

THE WONDERFUL WORLD
OF WORK

Happy is the man who loves his work, they say.
You'd think so, wouldn't you. It's Common Sense.

Not necessarily, though. This sort of thing is said by people who
haven't thought it through. The real reason to work is after all to
provide for yourself and your loved ones. But what about once
it's gone pear-shaped, and you're still expected to grind away
keeping her in the manner to which she was never really
accustomed, along with the three kids she's gone on to have
with that bloke you'd kill if you could? Then it would be a kind of
miserable torture doing a job you love with someone else reaping
the rewards, wouldn't it? The best bet in that situation would be
either to take a job you hate, so you can really get your teeth into
resenting every single penny you earn, or else a job that simply
doesn't allow you time to think. Mind you, you're probably not
the sort of bloke who's particularly happy whatever the
circumstances, are you, thinking about it.

THERE ARE TWO CRUCIAL THINGS TO
REMEMBER ABOUT WORK.

1) Always only ever do the bare minimum.[74]

2) See number 1. (I practise what I preach.)

---

[74] See *BARE MINIMUM, THE, DOING.*

Doesn't sound like much, but getting number one wrong will cause you far more grief than you can imagine.

The British workplace ticks along on a delicate balance, known as an equilibrium.[75]

Anyone who causes this equilibrium to be disturbed is playing with more than fire. There are five days in the week, never forget, so anyone who rushes ahead and does something today that would normally take him two or three days is simply proving how slack he'd been all along: whatever you do don't work too hard or you'll prove how hard you *can* work. Being too keen marks you out instantly as the workplace wanker, and which would you rather be: productive or popular? Exactly.

When you look at the world of work something becomes apparent pretty quickly, and that is in general, most people have no real idea what's going on in their company, and more specifically, what they're actually doing. Go into any workplace and check out the staggering amount of tooth-sucking, head-shaking, blank looks and general bewilderment.

The key is to look busy.

Ask a question that involves even a momentary glimpse of understanding of the operation they are paid to participate in, and you'll be buried under a mountain of blether, bluster, and buck-passing. People are just doing the bare minimum, getting

[75] Which actually comes from the Latin word meaning 'bare minimum'.

178

by, and if they don't absolutely need to know how something works, they won't know and won't be able to summon up the enthusiasm to guess. Add into this the fact that they're already trying to make a day's work cover three, and the chances of anything getting done at all in any major British workplace are fairly slender. And in a moment of crisis, most close their eyes and hope for the best.

Just look at a few examples: Doctors – no idea what they're doing. They wait for the nurses to do everything and hope to God no one dies, at least not while they're lying in a cot sleeping through their bleeper. There isn't a lawyer in the world who really knows what he's doing, and two thirds of his time is taken up with working out how much he's going to charge for it. Train drivers – they just keep going don't they? Hope for the best, sandwich in one hand, dead man's handle in the other, crossing their fingers at every level crossing. Airline pilots – well they rely on the autopilot to land the thing, and the autopilot was programmed by someone who doesn't really know what he's doing, because he was taught by someone who didn't really know what he was doing…airline pilots shut their eyes and hope for the best like the rest of us.

But whatever it is you do for a living, however it is you earn an honest crust, remember as you sit down in the pub at the end of the working day and take that first deep sip from the sweet lager of life, there's some bugger on the other side of the world going to work right this minute AND YOU'RE NOT!! HA HA LIFE IS SWEET!! RESULT!! GET IT DOWN YA!!![76]

[76]Though do bear in mind the reverse is true, that when you shuffle into work with a four quart hangover and a skin like a Rhino's hide that he's just sitting down to his first of the evening, and chances are where he is it's sunny.

THIS COULD SAVE YOUR LIFE ONE DAY

S.A.S. (SMASHED AND SLAUGHTERED)

I bloody love the S.A.S. Well, who doesn't? (Foreigners, that's who, and international terrorists and bad guys and villains and Bond baddy-style baddies, and even they have a grudging respect for the elitest elite-fighting elite force in the history of the planet.)

So when I decided to come up with a survival guide for how to survive when you are too pissed to make it all the way home, I thought: what better model could I use than S.A.S. tactics, S.A.S. techniques, and S.A.S. thinking?

Okay, here we go:
You! Yes, you! You've stayed in the pub until chucking out time, spent every last penny you possess on God's own British ale, and suddenly you find yourself cast out into the night, alone, broke, and bereft of the motor skills necessary to haul your sorry arse home to bed.

You make it as far as the car park, but can't identify your car, even though all the other cars have gone. You try the train station but the last train is smugly chugging out of view. So you decide you'll walk it. What the hell. It's only three and half miles.

This could be the last dumb decision you ever make.

Because make no mistake about it: it's a harsh and unforgiving wilderness out there.

Now you're on the street. The last bus has gone, and the chippy is shut. Taxis are veering across to the other side of the road to get away from you. You're cold, you're weary, and the will to live is ebbing away. Yet somewhere deep in your psyche a small flame still flickers, a small voice that whispers, 'No, I will not give in. I...want...to...survive!'

Congratulations! These Survival Tips are for you. Keep these close by, they could save your life. They have been arrived at through the time-honoured system of Learn and Error.

Now, in this first key period of semi-lucidity, your body will be trying to shut down, telling you to find somewhere to kip, but don't listen to it, not yet. First you have to take care of some essentials:

FIND WATER.

The Human Being[77] requires water to live, and also to stave off the jack-hammering hangover that is just around the corner.

---

[77] Don't know why I couldn't have just put 'people' or 'you' here, it's just The Human Being makes it sound more like I know what I'm on about.

A good source of water for the determined street staggerer is fast food detritus. Check the bins – actually, what am I talking about, bins are absolutely the last bloody place you'll find fast food detritus. Check out people's front gardens, gutters, the middle of the road, flower beds, on the floor next to the bin and the doorways of electrical goods stores. Anywhere but bins. What you are looking for is the discarded waxed cardboard cup for fizzy pop, ideally with lid and straw intact. More often than not, you will find these have been jettisoned with a handful of ice cubes left in the bottom. These melt, and are a handy source of H_2O that could buy you precious time. Also, polystyrene burger boxes catch rain water like nobody's business. And you might find a bit of chicken. Another good natural resource, later on, as the sun is coming up, is the early morning fitness freak. Maybe you are dozing on a park bench somewhere, your head is beginning to pound, and you wish you were dead, but it's well worth keeping a weather eye out for these fellas. What you are looking for is a good thick bush with plenty of foliage, something like a rhododendron, to conceal yourself in. When the fitness freak draws level with your position you strike like a cobra with a hangover, leap out, push him over and nick his water bottle.

Failing that, you may hear a council street-cleaning truck doing the rounds, in which case you could do worse than lie in the gutter with your mouth open. Not much worse, though.

KEEP WARM.

The booze will keep you warm for a while but beware: this will wear off. You need to use this grace time to find the specifics needed to keep the core body temperature[78] as high as possible, given it's the middle of the night. If you do not find warmth you may find you start to shiver, in which case: Do Not Panic! This is physiological regulation, and is just your muscles working overtime, trying to generate heat. Either that or it's the D.T.'s kicking in, in which case you're going to have more problems than just finding somewhere to keep warm. Good luck with that.

Newspapers are an excellent natural insulator. A normal tabloid when separated can cover a grown man, blanket fashion. Or you can stuff it into your clothes so it doesn't blow away. And now thanks to recycling, people actually sort their rubbish for you, to make it easier to get at the newspapers. God bless Greenpeace.[79] Also there's those free newspapers everywhere, aren't there, employing journalists who can't get paid work on proper papers (many of whom will be trying to kip nearby), so there's a bigger range than ever to choose from. *Metro*, for example, has a Tog rating of 5.5. Which is amazing seeing how little there is in it.

Ideally you are looking to find a nice combination: tabloid for warmth, broadsheet for coverage, and some kind of glossy grotmag or celebrity muckraker for rudimentary waterproofing.

---

[78]The temperature at which The Human Being is still capable of saying 'Cor!' when faced with an attractive member of the opposite sex.
[79]Except for when they're annoyingly banging on about global warming (see GLOBAL WARMING: DO YOUR BIT).

CAMOUFLAGE.

When you're trying to make it through to daybreak without paying your dues for the evening before, the last thing you want is to make a spectacle of yourself and get yourself nicked. A night in the cells can look pretty damn good at 3a.m. on a bitter and windswept January morning, and actually the breakfasts aren't bad either, but you've made it this far and you owe it to yourself to see it through.

So. You must learn to blend into the shadows, to become not *in* the night but *of* the night. This means no walking down the white lines in the middle of the street singing *Unchained Melody* at top volume, however good you reckon you are at the high bit. Time, place. The time for that is Karaoke Night, and the place is somebody else's pub.

This means no going round to your ex-girlfriend's house and waking everyone up by kicking the empty milk bottles while you try to find the doorbell.

If you are going to survive, you need to learn not to draw attention to yourself. You need to learn how to hide, to lurk, to camouflage yourself, to disappear. Here's a good tip. Every other shop in every High Street in the country now seems to be a charity shop of some kind. Do-gooders are always leaving great piles and bin liners full of old clothes outside them for the part-time biddies who work there to sort through in the morning before burning them.

These are, by the way, well worth checking out as a source of vital extra layers. That's not the tip, though. That's this: if you spot a representative of Her Majesty's police force approaching, it is – with the proper training and practice – the work of a moment to transform yourself into something resembling one of these piles. The trick is not just to look right, though, it's to *believe* it. Think to yourself: 'I *am* the pile, I *am* the pile ...' Chances are after a night on the lash your kit is going to look more or less second hand, and the smell will deter closer inspection, with a bit of luck. With practice and self-denial it's possible to attain such a state of oneness with a pile of old clothes that the experienced street staggerer will not even flinch when prodded with a truncheon or pissed on by a police Alsatian.

Just make sure you don't try doing this outside WHSmith's or something. The key to good camouflage, you see, is not to be as thick as two short planks (unless you're trying to conceal yourself in a miniature lumber yard of some kind).

SLEEP.

All right: you've found some water, collected some insulation, and avoided detection by the boys in blue. You're ready to start looking for a place to get some kip.

Here are some options:

The Park. This is a little obvious, and for that reason you may find you have strong competition for the prime locations, by which I mean the benches erected in memory of someone who loved this spot, and the bandstand, which has a roof on it and consequently needs bagsying mid-afternoon to have any realistic chance of a berth. The full-time tramp population, you see, they've got it all sewn up. It's not what you know, but who you know.

Shop Doorways. See The Park (above).

Telephone Box. The old-style red ones are great at keeping the cold out, and if you are able to sleep standing up then they are the perfect place to stay until morning (though it can be a royal pain in the arse when the tiny windows have been smashed out exactly next to where your kidneys are and you get a draft in the exact spot you don't need one). Remember to wedge the receiver under your ear so it looks like you're using the box for its proper purpose, and to smash the mechanism so it doesn't make that bloody irritating 'Hang Me Up!' noise. If you can't kip this way then you will 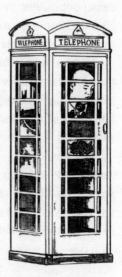 find you've committed yourself to standing in a glass cubicle for five or six hours waiting for morning to break. Which can be a bit on the bleak side of bleak. Still, nobody said survival was going to be easy.

Crazy Like A Fox. The park, shop doorways, telephone boxes. They're good, but they're not particularly S.A.S., are they? So try this one:

Any survivalist will tell you: be like the fox, the fox is smart. If you're freezing your arse off, then take a tip from Monsieur[80]

[80]French word.

Reynard, he knows what he's doing. He's an expert at finding a sheltered spot, away from prying eyes, where he can dig himself into a cosy little burrow, with leaves and moss acting as Mother Nature's Blanket. Most towns are rotten with foxes these days – urban foxes, they're called – and so it shouldn't take too long for you to spot one loping along between the parked cars. Follow him – not too close, you'll scare him off, remember, he's clever, old Foxy – let him take his time, let him lead you to his lair, his nice, cosy, moss-lined, sheltered lair. When you're certain you've found it – maybe it's in a park, or in someone's back garden, or along a railway line, or in a rubbish tip (he's brainy is old urban Foxy, he's got street smarts) – then you creep up, slowly, closer and closer, easy does it, until you're sure the moment is right, then... RUSH HIM! Making as much racket as possible! Foxy will run off, and you grab his nice warm bed. Ha! Stupid fox...

Wheelie Bins. Grab a wheelie bin, drag it to a quiet spot, kick it over, tip all the rubbish out, climb in, cover yourself with newspaper, and forty winks are yours for the taking. The main thing to be wary of is busybodies tipping the bin back up and dragging it back to where you nicked it from with you still inside it. For this reason avoid

bins that have house numbers painted on them – those people will do anything to get 'their' wheelie bins back. Oh, and don't use this tip on a Tuesday – you might wake up on a refuse barge heading out into the Irish Sea (and our survival tips don't cover that, you're on your own mate).

HOME SWEET HOME: GET YOUR STORY STRAIGHT.

If you've made it this far you've done the hard yards, but it is by no means over. You may well have dodged the pneumonia and the arrest (cardiac and constabulary). But there's one final obstacle that could make this whole ordeal utterly futile. You must now face…the other half. Please read this final section carefully. Then re-read it.

When you are caught sneaking into the kitchen at half past eight a.m., in your drinking suit with fox dirt all over the back of it, a copy of Metro sticking out of your Calvin Kleins, an empty bumper Diet Tango carton in one hand, and some jogger's iPod in the other, then make sure you have something up your sleeve (apart from bits of grass and dead leaves) that's better than this:

'Oh, hullo luv, I really caned it last night – any chance of a brew?'

Maybe this accurately reflects the events of the previous evening, and your needs at that moment, but this is a Survival Guide, and that sort of thing, believe me, will get you your nuts cut off and handed to you in a bag, and not the bag they belong in. Ouch.

Any time you can put in preparing for this crisis-point will be golden, I promise you. Learn this and you should be able to turn things around:

'Oh, hullo luv ... I'd just got in last night – you were asleep, I tried really hard not to wake you – and I thought I heard a noise, so I came downstairs, and there was a burglar, yes, that's it, a burglar.

188

I chased him into the garden, and slipped on some fox dirt, and you wouldn't believe the litter out there, bloody kids, coh! And I caught him, and we struggled, but I must have hit me head or something because he got away, still at least I managed to stop him from nicking ... this iPod I bought you ... for our anniversary!'

That's the sort of thing you're looking for. Heroic, yet thoughtful, and impossible to disprove. You can have that one. Remember, if you do balls up this bit, there's a fair chance you won't be able to go out and do it all again that night. Which after all is the object of the exercise.

☞ **THE WAY THINGS ARE**

<u>No. 4: Life's Tough</u>

Life's tough, no matter how gifted you might be. Like the way that Captain Sensible never made it to Major, despite his many years of loyal service. There's every chance it might not happen.

EXTRA 4-PLY DURABLE

SAVE!

JESUS CHRIST, (0-?),
Messiah, King of the Jews, chippie, said:

'Live each day as if it's your last'

Sounds good doesn't it? But, it's not very practical advice is it? And it could go either way: you could see it as an opportunity to make up to everyone for all the wrong doing you've done, a chance to make amends, for penitence, confession, contrition. Or you could see it as a chance to get off your face. And nine times out of ten that's what people are going to do. And if you were living each day as if it's your last 365 days of the year you'd end up a nervous wreck. Nice one Jesus, you didn't think it through.

❖

TOP TWENTY SITCOMS WHERE THE TITLE IS A LOAD-BEARING PUN ON THE LEAD CHARACTER'S NAME

Common Sense highlights the fact there's too many sitcoms. They are piling up most of them, languishing unwatched and there's no way there's enough time to trawl through them all.

They should have stopped making them after they made *Brittas Empire*, which is probably the second greatest sitcom ever made. The second? I hear you ask. Yes, everyone knows that *Fawlty Towers* is the greatest situation comedy television programme ever made. Many have tried to recreate the magic, and all but a few have failed. Why is it so good? That's the question. Great characters, naturally. Funny plots, goes without saying. Hilarious consequences, but of course. Ripping the piss out of the Germans, the French, the Americans and the Spanish – that's a bonus. The real keystone of Cleese's genius, though – and this is a tip for all you budding comedical writers out there – is this. His character's name is in the title, and – wait for it – it's also a pun. Fawlty, you see. It's his name, but it also sounds like 'faulty', which means gone wrong. So the Towers are not only Fawlty, they're also faulty. That's the beauty of it. It's so bursting with comedy goodness that there's even a joke in the title. And he can move the letters around on the sign so it says Flowery Twats.

Now some of the best and most successful sitcoms have tried to follow where the mighty Cleese has trod, but they've invariably cocked it up. The Americans have many sit-coms that, we are forever being told, are better than ours, though how can I laugh at a gag about a Twinky when I don't know what a Twinky is? What is a Twinky? Anyone? But let's take *Frasier*, for example. It's very clever, I'm sure, and the title has the character's name in it, but it's not a pun, is it, not by any stretch. See, if they'd called it something like Well Known Frasier Sayings, or Frasier Jolly Good Fellow it'd have been a pun, and maybe people wouldn't have got tired of it so quickly. *Seinfeld*, another Yank show, has its admirers, but the character's name and the actor's name are the same name as the programme, which is needlessly confusing and an opportunity gone begging. What about Thank You Jerry Much, eh? That would have worked much better and that's just off the top of my head.

The sitcoms on the following list, however, have managed to strike comedy gold, and if you can't remember them they must have got one of the other bits wrong, like characterisation, plotting or not putting any jokes in, because you just can't fault those punny titles. Hold onto your sides – this is how it's done:

IMMANUEL KANT (1724–1804)

German philosopher, said

'Out of the crooked tree of humanity,
no straight thing can be made'

Oh yeah? What about a cricket bat? That's pretty straight. Just off the top of my head...

■ **The Brittas Empire** His name is Mr Brittas, and he runs a sports centre. That's his empire. Brittas isn't really even a real name – looked in the phone book, not one single Brittas, not one – it's just totally made up because it sounds a bit like British. The British Empire. They could have called him Mr British, but tweaked it just that extra little gnat's. Genius. *See Todays Choice.* ★★★★☆

2.00 Chance In A Million In which the main character is called Tom Chance, and he's a blinking oddball, hence he's one in a million. So it's a pun, and it's the bloke's name. Couldn't be more impressed. Why it sank without trace I'll never know.

3.00 Every Silver Lining Nat Silver and Shirley Silver are a bickering Jewish couple running a café somewhere in the East End of London. With hilarious consequences. It had Manuel in it, and he'd clearly been paying attention when Cleese was spreading the comedy wisdom about during the breaks in rehearsals. Although, thinking about it, they made a bit of a botch up of the phrase or saying, which is 'every cloud has a silver lining', isn't it. That's why he's always the sidekick, you see, and never the kick.

4.00 Faith In The Future Her name is Faith, and she has faith, you see, in what the future will bring. Or else it was set in the future. Can't really remember ... but that's not the point, the point is the title is a load-bearing pun, and that's what counts.

TODAY'S CHOICE

Mr Brittas: we'll never see his like again.

5.00 Fresh Fields A middle-aged couple are trying to get some new excitement in their life, looking for pastures new, if you will, or (at a stretch) fresh fields. And their name is Fields. They weren't themselves particularly fresh, but we'll let that go. Where they did cross the line, though, was with the sequel, where the Fields up sticks and go and live in France. French Fields, it was called, which isn't a pun on anything except the title of their own original show, which in my view is cheating.

■ **The Good Life** They're a suburban couple giving up the rat race to follow their dream, which is to cultivate their suburban garden and somehow make themselves self-sufficient with a goat and a couple of chickens. That's the good life bit, but then check out their names. He's Tom Good, and she's Barbara Good. I think there was another one called Ebenezer Good, but I may have remembered that wrong.

7.00 Grace And Favour Clever, this one. It's about grace and favour accommodation, which to be honest is an infrequently occuring phenomenon these days, provided for the staff of Grace Brothers, by young Mr Grace, as a favour. A sequel to another show that wasn't a pun title show – clearly they saw where they had been going wrong with that Are You Being Served? thing all those years.

8.00 Grace Under Fire A person can show grace under fire, it's a bona fide barely-used phrase or saying. How much better though that the main character is a woman whose name is Grace. And she is under fire – not literally, like with guns or something, but beset by life's little problems, sort of thing. So it just about worked. Sounded the death knell for that Are You Being Served? sequel where they all go back and fire bomb the department store in revenge for leaving them all on the scrapheap, though. Perhaps for the best.

9.00 The House That Jack Built- Adam Faith is a builder called Jack. He has built a house. Where's the pun? They've just taken the well-known phrase or saying, and given their character the name out of it, without adding any layers of humour to it at all. Lazy, but along the right lines.

10.00 Not On Your Nellie You might say this well-known phrase if you were in the old days before there was swearing and you wanted to say no to something with extra emphasis. It was also a sitcom with Hylda Baker in it, and she played someone called Nellie who didn't like having things put on her. In the old days.

11.00 The Nutt House Not a show about a mental institution, as the name might lead you to believe, but a sitcom about a hotel, run by a Mr and Mrs Nutt. Why was this not the new Fawlty Towers? I don't understand it. All the ingredients were in place. Back to the drawing board, fellers...

MORE CHOICES OVERLEAF>>

■ George and the Dragon

Sid James was George, the chauffeur for some posh nob, and Peggy Mount was the housekeeper for same. They called her Gabrielle Dragon, in order to make the title work, and to let you know which were the two main characters in it. See *picture opposite* ★★★☆☆

13.00 Mann's Best Friends

Henry Mann has some friends. With hilarious consequences, probably derived from the fact that you're expecting them to be dogs, but they turn out to be people. Two 'N's in Mann, you see. Not the well-known phrase and saying Man's Best Friend, meaning dog, at all. Mr Mackay was in it, off of Porridge (great show, crap title by the way).

✳ 14.00 Nelson's Column

The main bloke is called Gavin Nelson, and he works on a local paper, where he writes a column. See what they did there? It seems to be about a famous London landmark, but in fact it's a sitcom about a newspaper. Plus it had that really tall thin Scotsman in it that they get whenever they need a put-upon nerd type, who looks a bit like a stone column. And yet this isn't on any more either.

15.00 A Prince Among Men

In this one the main character was a footballer called Gary Prince, and many of the other characters were men, so the well known phrase or saying 'a prince among men' worked a treat when it came to summing this up. Despite the fact that Prince was played by Mr Brittas (not one in the phone

book!), and punning wordplay was all over that title, which seems to be what they want, for crying out loud, the powers that be flushed this one down the bog as well. They don't know what they're doing up there, I'm telling you …

16.00 Robin's Nest

The main character is a chef called Robin, which is the same name as a bird, which lives in a nest, so he called his restaurant Robin's Nest. Hence the title. Had that bloke in it who was the washer-up with one arm who was also in Fawlty Towers as the Irish builder (with two arms – how did he do that?).

17.00 Land Of Hope And Gloria

Lots of points for this one, though, look. One of the characters, the really posh English bloke, was called Hope, and the other one, the brassy American woman who comes to manage his posh estate, she's called Gloria. So there's a Hope, and a Gloria, and it's about some land. Plus, they've slightly changed the title of a well-known song, which is top class pun work. For some

Above:. Wendy Craig. Unlucky.   Unless it's Mr Gary Prince, played by the same bloke.

reason, though, it was only ever on that one time, even though it had the bird with the huge mouth off of the Three Degrees in it, which should have made it a sure-fire winner.

18.00 Roman's Empire An attempt to recreate the Brittas magic. A bloke called Roman has a business empire, with hilarious consequences. To my mind they haven't put in the hard yards on the character's name here. If they'd gone for The Romas Empire, it might have stood half a chance.

19.00 Running Wild Max Wild, played by the bloke who used to be Mr Benn who is now a murderer on EastEnders, yearns to rediscover his youth, hence he's running wild. Do you get it? He's running, he's

called Wild, he's running wild. You can absolutely see what they were trying for. If only it had been funnier I'm sure I'd remember more about it, with a cracking title like that one.

■ **Laura and Disorder**
She's a middle-aged divorcee called Laura, and her life is in a mess, which is where the disorder comes in. And it's a pun on the phrase Law and Order, in which they've changed both the main words, leaving only the 'and' intact. Despite this textbook titling, Wendy Craig only got six episodes out of this one, and yet that other one, Butterflies, where she was a terrible cook and the title didn't have any jokes in it at all, seemed to be on for ever. *See picture above* ★★★★★

The Olde Gods

Nowadays no one believes in much it's fair to say, no one goes to Church and no one believes a word they say on the news etc., etc. In fact the only belief that people cling to nowadays is the belief that no one believes in anything any more. Unbelievable. But actually I think that we all, deep down, do believe in something, something ancient and powerful, something that, even if we know it or not, we believe in, in our guts.

I am of course talking about the Olde Gods, the Ancient Anglo Saxon Gods, who were here long before the Christian Church arrived on these shores. Ancient Gods who we call to in times of crisis, ancient powerful deities whose names tie us to this land through our language. When the moment comes we call upon these Gods, invoke them and wait for their incomparable power and justice to shine through. Their names are known to all, yet some dare not even utter their names, children are told not to say them, and old ladies quake and tremble when they hear them. Their names cannot be said on television until after nine o'clock. In fact, so powerful are their names we dare not print them for fear of the forces we might unleash: we are using subtle symbols to conceal, yet hint at their identities. This has been done for you, the reader's, safety.

But who are these Ancient Gods? Behold the pantheon, for lo, their names are known to us all:

F⁻©k - The god of good fortune who looks over all. Thank F⁻©k for that!' we cry when fortune smiles upon us. F⁻©k as the father of the Olde Gods rules all he surveys, and when he smiles upon us we thank him. And we get on with our little lives here below, for F⁻©k's sake. In Ireland he was known as Feck, and in the south of England he is sometimes called Fack, in the North Fook, but he is essentially the same. And when our time comes, wherever we hail from, and we are summoned to meet the gods face to face, we know we will all have gone to F⁻©k.

Co©k - The impish god of mayhem, a malicious little sprite that pops up at inappropriate moments to thwart your best endeavours. Oh Co©k!'we cry, 'I've co©ked that up!', little knowing that we are harking back to the phrase's ancient meaning, which is to introduce mayhem to a situation. Usually depicted as really small, although his followers believed that actually he was massive. Except when he'd just been swimming.

The Olde Gods

Bo££o©ks - The curly-haired god of Truth. Even now, even though centuries have passed since Bo££o©ks worship was popular up and down the land, you hear his name invoked. Whenever some smug chancer tries to tell you something that is palpably untrue, for example, Bo££o©ks!' we say, calling on the ancient divinity to shine the light of truth into the dispute, Bo££o©ks!' we cry in court when the copper calls our son a thief.

B¯gge® - The dark god, the god of confusion, the god of making the best of a bad situation. How often, even now, we find ourselves half-way through something, and it's not going well, and we can't summon up the will or the enthusiasm to complete the thing properly, do we find ourselves exclaiming, 'Oh, B¯gge® this...' and going to see what's on telly.

T!t - The queen of the ancient Gods, who sits by F¯©k's right hand, and takes care of women's problems. In olden times - or tymes, as they used to be called - women were not allowed to mention the names of the senior male gods or to invoke them in prayer, which has led to the reticence we can still see today. The name of T!t, however, they were happy to make free with. What a useless t!t!' they might have said about some bloke, carrying the ancient meaning: 'He is no help at all with women's problems.'

P®!©k - The god of Hubris. Proud is the P®!©k, standing tall, inviting ridicule, showing us that pride can only lead to one place, a fall. The instant you see someone beset with pride the word 'P®!©k!' springs to your lips - again you are invoking the name of an Olde God.

**P!$$** - A rollicking raucous olde god, the god of drinking and good times - or tymes. P!$$ is usually depicted flat on his back, or waving a jug or a tankard around, so even now if you organise 'a bit of a p!$$ up', at which you 'get p!$$ed', you are paying tribute to this ancient deity. His followers were known as 'the p!$$heads', and were generally too slammed to do anything, which is why no temples remain standing - they never managed to finish any.

W@^k - The ancient god of Guilt, who has always had an enthusiastic following of young male adherents, many of whom would devote themselves to acts of worship several times a day. These young men, collectively known as 'W@^kers', would dream of the day they could escape the clutches of their lord W@^k, and graduate to becoming fully-fledged F¯©kers.

PUB QUIZ CRIB SHEET (1) – FOOTBALL CLUB NICKNAMES

A fine institution, is the Pub Quiz Night, devised – like so many pub activities – with a view to creating as many losers as possible.

The thinking there, you see, is that the pub will then be packed out with people determined to drink away their sorrow and humiliation or else indulge in misery feasting on your hot and cold bar snacks. It can be a bonanza at the tills, I'm telling you.

Not like bloody karaoke –'Oh, just a glass of tepid tap water, please, I have to take care of my vocal chords!' Time wasters...

So. The following resource may be used whether you are:

(a) A PUB LANDLORD (in which case I salute you, always providing you have a dartboard) wishing to create the optimum pub quiz for Pub Quiz Night.

OR

(b) A DRINKER (in which case, again, I salute you, always providing you observe the rules, and partake of ale [*male*] or white wine/fruit-based drink [*female*], as is right and proper) wishing to get one up on the table of nerds who only show up on Pub Quiz Night and manage to make one pint of Ribena and lemonade last the whole evening.

At any pub quiz on any Pub Quiz Night anywhere in the world there will, as sure as eggs is eggs (and they is, I assure you –

extensive tests have been made and the proof is pretty much universally accepted nowadays), be a question, or questions, or maybe even a whole round, about Football Club Nicknames.

So what, you say. And indeed, as far as *English* Football Club Nicknames are concerned, this is a fairly straightforward area. The club has a nickname, usually some thought has gone into it, to wit:

PUB QUIZ CRIB SHEET

CRIB SHEET No. 3

TOPIC ENGLISH FOOTBALL CLUB NICKNAMES

CLUB	NICKNAME	WHY?
ARSENAL	The Gunners	It's an arsenal. It's got guns in it. It's not hard.
LIVERPOOL	The Reds	They play in red. What's the problem? It's Common Sense.
MAN UTD	The Red Devils	They play in red, and always win, so they must have made some sort of pact with Satan.
NORWICH CITY	The Canaries	They play in yellow. They look like canaries.
ASTON VILLA	The Villians	A made-up word that sounds like villains – the clue's in the name.
TOTTENHAM HOTSPUR	Spurs	The clue's in the name.
WEST HAM	The Hammers	The clue's in the name.
FULHAM	The Cottagers	I was never confused.
MILLWALL	The Lions	Grrr... Scary.
HULL CITY	The Tigers	See above. Plus they play in yellow and black.
WOLVERHAMPTON WANDERERS	Wolves	See above. Plus the clue's in the name.
BRIGHTON & HOVE ALBIONH	The Seagulls	It's by the sea. It's not hard. They've just got no imagination.
NEWCASTLE UTD	The Magpies	They play in black and white.
SUNDERLAND	The Black Cats	They play in red and white...no, hang on...Sunderland is famous for its... or it's the capital city of the cats. Especially the black ones Or something...

'I'M ONLY HUMAN...'

Of all the expressions, the one that makes me weary and fills me with despair, is the expression 'only human'. Because for my money there is nothing 'only' about being human. People say that when they're making excuses. Sorry love, I knobbed that bird because I'm Only Human. I ate that cake because I'm Only Human. I was sick in the glove compartment because I'm Only Human.

There's nothing 'only' about being human, nothing at all. Human beings are truly amazing, and have done some amazing things. Being human is about landing on the moon, going to the bottom of the ocean, going down the pub. If you're calling that 'only' human, then what are you saying is better? I suppose some fish have been to the bottom of the deepest ocean, the creepy transparent-looking ones, but take them up a mountain and they won't look so pleased with themselves. Human beings are truly amazing, and alright we are told that chimps can use sticks as spears, but you know what, we can fly and compute[81] and read and do brain surgery[82] and all those other things which beat waggling a stick at another monkey.

Alright dogs and chimps have been into space, I suppose, but they didn't do it by themselves, did they? No, humans threw them up there, and got them back too (most of them).

[81] Well, maybe not me, but you see the point I'm making.
[82] And again.

203

Animals? Don't make me laugh (apart from on the *You've Been Framed Animals Getting Hurt Specials*). Humans, though, have a sense of humour. Most of us anyway. I'm not including the bloke who thought of *Noel's House Party*.[83] But animals don't have a sense of humour, do they? Hyenas aren't really laughing. At best they're sneering in a sardonic fashion. Monkeys are around bananas every single day of their lives but not once do they put down a skin for another one to slip on. Timewasters, the gag's right there begging to be done! Dolphins – po-faced bunch of bottle-nosed bastards! They take life far too seriously, don't they, the humourless bunch of do-gooding gits – hanging around with the sick and the thin. They sleep with their eyes open – do you know any human who sleeps with his eyes open? No. And if you did would you trust him? No. They're totally overrated, dolphins, they're not that smart, are they?[84]

The point is, humans are great. The human condition is not a disease. Even though it sounds like one. And it's not just technological achievements. Think of the humble bigamist. In order to follow what seem like 'only' human urges he has to live the most complex life imaginable. All those lies, the endless web of complication and deceit, the imagination required to keep the whole thing spinning. Twice the dinners too, hence the name bigamist, because he's bigger than most. A man with twelve wives would be called a dodecadigamist I suppose, how fat would he be? And all because he is 'only' human.

[83] Noel.
[84] Einstein didn't do tricks for fish, did he? Mind you, if he had, eh? What a great all-rounder he'd have been.

DR WHO – WHO'S BETTER WHO'S BETTER WHO'S BEST?

Though *Dr Who* is for kids, there is no doubt that the silly old time-travelling bigger-on-the-inside gent is part of the fabric of our British culture, whether we like it or not.

Any pub conversationalist must be equipped for the inevitable conversation that will arise should the subject surface like the pong from a nerd's recently disturbed week-old socks. It's a simple conversation, that never really extends further than the simple question of Who[85] is the best Doctor. Easily done this one. So, in no particular order:

1. **Troughtnell/Hartnon.** All in black and white, reminds me of a French film, so I tend to give those fellas a wide berth, force of habit, nothing personal. Of course the BBC wiped most of the tapes, apparently. But they must have been good because they led to Pertwee, Who[86] led to Baker.

2. **Jon Pertwee.** With his cuffs and kung fu moves and vintage motor, also top flight. Despite his slight lisp. But did you know he was French??

[85] Convention demands that throughout this next bit the word Who always has a capital W.
[86] See? Tedious, isn't it?

3. **Tom Baker.** Who[87] can forget the scarf, the toothy smile, the jelly-babies, K9, Stavros etc., etc? There's no point even going on about this, he's the best and it proves itself, I'm not going to waste valuable drinking time arguing this one out.

4. **Peter Davidson,** Jim's brother ('Nick nick!' – they can't replace stars like that can they?) sadly lacked the necessary gravitas to play the errant Timelord on account of his not being a bit mental bla bla…lost interest, sorry, I'd after all given up halfway through Tom to be honest. It's for kids.

5. **Colin Baker.** Trying to bring back the Baker magic by casting another Baker. Apparently it was either him or Cheryl Baker out of *Buck's Fizz*. By this time I was well into my teens and girls had hoved into view.

6. **Sylvester McCoy.** Moving on.

7. **One of the McGanns** in that movie. Nerds doubt whether it's 'canon', in other words whether it counts as an official *Dr Who* story. Imagine worrying about something like that. Christ.

8. **Christopher Ecclestone.** The man who brought it all back, reinvented the whole thing, wore a leather jacket, shouted a bit, then quit. Something the whole family could sit down and watch together, I haven't seen my boy for eight years now, thanks for bringing that up you big-eared Northern acting ponce.

9. **The current one, Tennants.** Very strong, skinny. Like him a lot. Even. Though. It's. For. Kids.[88]

10. **Sean Connery** is the best James Bond. No arguing.

And that's all you need know about Dr Who, and we knocked this one off in far less time than James bloody Bond.

[87] Sick of it.

[88] As is the spin off, *Touchcloth*, even though it has swearing in it, and lesbians.

PUB QUIZ CRIB SHEET (2) – SCOTTISH FOOTBALL CLUB NICKNAMES

Now, unlike the BBC, I am actually aware of the fact that there are football matches occurring north of the border and that the teams and results mean something to the people living there.

On the other hand these teams don't follow any straightforward thinking when it comes to their nicknames, but that's the Jocks for you.

Some Scottish Club Nicknames can be arrived at fairly simply. They're just the last syllable of the team name, grunted in your classic Scots manner, possibly while waving a haggis pie and a can of Tennents. So Rangers, for example, are Gers. Not an ounce of fat on that nickname. Motherwell are Well, Dundee are Dee, and Morton are Ton. Poetry. Others, though, defy rational explanation, which is why they keep cropping up in pub quizzes, of course.

Take a look at this little lot, learn and inwardly digest:

Jim Bowen in the middle of a bully wee: see overleaf

PUB QUIZ CRIB SHEET

CRIB SHEET NO. 2

TOPIC Scottish Football Club Nicknames

CLUB	NICKNAME	WHY?
CLYDE	The Bully Wee	Is it just me, or does this conjure up an unsettling image of Jim Bowen on the toilet...?
FALKIRK	The Bairns	This is Scottish talk for babies. The Babies, they call themselves. How inspiring is that?
ST MIRREN	The Buddies	Ah they're all buddies. Grow up.
FORFAR ATHLETIC	The Lōōns	I think I see the thinking here, although it is unexpectedly self-aware.
CELTIC	The Bhoys	Well, fine, as long as you don't find yourself playing against a team made up of Mhen.
STENHOUSMUIR	The Warriors	That's more like it.
DUNFERMLINE ATHLETIC	The Pars	Lot of golf courses in Scotland, and this is clearly a club with mediocre aspirations. Why not the Eagles? Well, because then they'd be Crystal Palace. But they might as well call themselves the Below Pars and have done with it.
AYR UND	The Honest Men	An admirable quality, honesty, although it is rather pointing the finger at everyone else. We're not diving, we're not claiming throw-ins when we know we booted the ball out. Sanctimonious p®!©ks.[89]

[89] See THE OLD GODS

CRIB SHEET No. 2

TOPIC SCOTTISH FOOTBALL CLUB NICKNAMES

CLUB	NICKNAME	WHY?
QUEEN'S PARK	The Spiders	If you're going to name yourself after a creature, at least make it one that's going to sound a little bit daunting and not a creepy-crawly. This nickname is, frankly, only going to scare ladies. You might as well have chosen the Little Tiny Mice.
HEARTS OF MIDLOTHIAN	The Jam Tarts	Named not after a mighty predator, such as might strike terror into the hearts of their enemies, but after a small, individual, lidless pie.
ARBROATH	The Red Lichties	Well, presumably they play in red, but what the hell is a lichtie? We'd really lichtie win a game every noo and then...? Make an effort!
QUEEN OF THE SOUTH	 The Doonhammers	For a start, lads, you're the Queen of the North – we've already got a Queen down here – and then you're just making up words. Do you mean Doom Hammers? That would be quite a good nickname, actually ... The Hammers of Doom. A bit like West Ham, only with more Doom.
DUNDEE UTD	THE TERRORS	Now you're talking.
STIRLING ALBION	THE BINOS	Can't even spell 'Winos'. That's how pissed they are.
SCOTLAND	THE JOCKS	It's a timeless classic – why quibble with it?

The Conquest Of The Normans

Ten Sixty-Six. The one blemish on an otherwise spotless record of military supremacy stretching back very nearly a whole millennium, spanning thwarted armadas and blunted blitzes. It's always stuck in my craw, that one, I have to admit.

However, that was before I thought it through. Because the thing I've come to realise is that the Normans, well, they're us, aren't they? They're the ones who turned out to be the Brits in the end. Of course they are. They won.

Norman is such a British name, isn't it, eh? That should have been the clue. We all know a Norman, don't we? He lives in a semi, drives an estate car and works in a biscuit factory. Has a couple of pints on a Saturday and watches *Match of the Day*, and never gives the wife – whose name is Audrey – a slap. He goes on holiday to a British beach resort, Norman does, and he sits on a deckchair with a knotted hanky on his head and his trousers rolled up eating fish and chips. Has a favourite pullover. Salt of the earth.

Back in Ten Sixty-Six the northern part of France was swarming with Normans, and they were like fish out of water, poor chaps, with their willingness to work hard and their inability to take a tan. Is it any wonder then, that all these Normans started to cast envious glances across the channel to a green and pleasant land where the food wasn't quite so garlicky and the farmers were a shade less bolshy? Where the weather was unpredictable, yes, but generally mild. Where the bread was sliced, and then fried with an egg on it. Where the men drank beer, and not wine. Where you could get a nice cup of tea. Imagine them all, peering through the mist, trying to spot the white cliffs of Dover, like a bunch of eleventh-century asylum seekers. They hated it in France, that's a fact, and they wanted something better.

For some time Britain had been ruled by mostly unimpressive kings with no backbones. Cnut, for example, a man who was just a single typographical error away from being the rudest footnote in history, drowned himself trying to order the sea around. Ethelred the Unready – how did he ever get the gig, that's what I don't understand.

'Time for your coronation, sire.'

'Hang on, I can't find my lucky pants...'

Harfacnut, who was only half as impressive as Cnut, if you can believe it. And Edward the Confessor, who was totally unable to ever win a battle on account of the fact that he would always give the plan of attack away to anyone who asked. And finally there was Harold, who got Edward to promise him the throne with this simple ruse:

'I'm going to be next king, aren't I, come on, own up.'

'Yes Harold, I admit it, I cannot tell a lie...'

These numpties, by and large, were Saxons, and it will come as no surprise to you to learn that Saxony is a part of **Germany**.

The Modern Day Norman

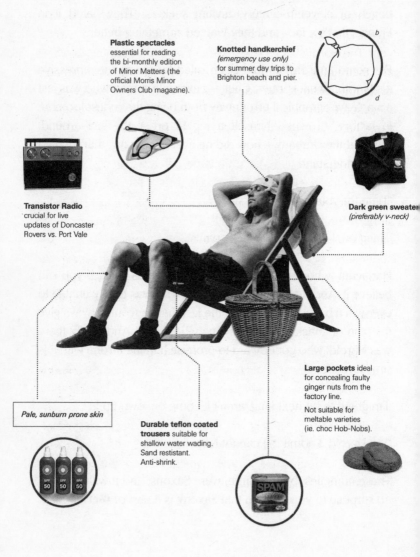

Plastic spectacles
essential for reading the bi-monthly edition of Minor Matters (the official Morris Minor Owners Club magazine).

Knotted handkerchief
(emergency use only)
for summer day trips to Brighton beach and pier.

Transistor Radio
crucial for live updates of Doncaster Rovers vs. Port Vale

Dark green sweater
(preferably v-neck)

Pale, sunburn prone skin

Durable teflon coated trousers suitable for shallow water wading. Sand restistant. Anti-shrink.

Large pockets ideal for concealing faulty ginger nuts from the factory line.

Not suitable for meltable varieties (ie. choc Hob-Nobs).

The Normans were led by William the Bastard. A lot of people think he was called William the Conqueror, but he hadn't conquered anything yet, and Bastard was his pre-conquering nickname. A good nickname was half the battle in them days. I mean, Unready – you wouldn't even bother turning up, would you? The Normans came across the Channel with their duty free and their horses on the old-fashioned trot-on-trot-off ferries and landed at Hastings. Harold was away because he'd arranged to meet some Norwegians at Stamford Bridge, but straight after the game he came down to Hastings for the bundle.

When the battle got under way, William pretended to run away, and Harold chased him, then William turned around and shot him in the eye. What a bastard, eh? Then he sold his exclusive story of the battle to the tapestries and went to London to get himself crowned king. Meanwhile all the other Normans set about subduing the hopeless 𝕲𝖊𝖗𝖒𝖆𝖓 Saxons, and making the Britain we know and love today, setting a sequence of events in motion that would ultimately lead to cribbage and the Morris Minor.

So when you think it through, in fact we weren't conquered at all in Ten Sixty-Six. It was a bunch of weedy and inept 𝕲𝖊𝖗𝖒𝖆𝖓𝖘 who shouldn't even have been here who got the kicking they richly deserved, while we, the Normans, who turned out to be British, were the winners yet again. Another great victory for us, in other words. So actually we haven't been conquered since the Romans in 43 AD, which is nearly two whole millenniums. Not too shabby.

WHY MEN HAD TO INVENT EQUALITY TO MAKE THINGS FAIRER

It's not Common Sense to make sweeping and inaccurate generalisations and I wouldn't also want to sound like I'm behind the times (I know what an iPod is) but men work and women stay at home, normally, usually, most of the time. I'm not saying this is fair but that's just the way things are. Okay there are some exceptions to the rule, let's not forget those part-time secretaries and nurses that help make this country what it is, great, normally, usually, most of the time.

In recent years there's been a blur in the roles, it's not always wise. Sometimes men do the hoovering and women do stuff that men do, like going to the pub and the football, again not always wise, we only need to look to history to see this. The first time a woman went to the races she threw herself in front of a horse – now I'm not sure if this was on purpose, she might have been trying to cross the course to get to the funfair, this has never been properly cleared up (though *she* was, oof, nasty) but it was nevertheless careless.

Actual Photo.

SO WHY IS THIS SO?

Simple, there's a reason for everything and the reason that men go out to work during the day and women don't is 'Daytime Television'. There was nothing on during the day but programmes about decorating or losing weight. So off to work men went keeping out of the house while David Dickinson flirted with two menopausal women in red jumpers. Then off to the pub to hide out as *Changing Rooms* draws to a close and the coast is clear for the start of *Where Eagles Dare* at 11.20pm. I mean how is a man supposed to sit through *Loose Women* except on the toilet reading *AutoTrader*? The name alone is a promise broken.

But since they started showing programmes like *Quincy*, the one with the bloke out of *Mary Poppins* in pretending to be a doctor, and *Inspector Morse*, there's been a significant shift in our culture: men don't mind staying at home. Now there is no need to go to work, if they are showing decent stuff during the day, normally, usually, most of the time (etc.).

WHY WOMEN ARE NOW EXPECTED TO PULL THEIR WEIGHT (BUT WHATEVER YOU DO DON'T MENTION THEIR WEIGHT)

How did the change come about?

It changed because we have this thing which is a bit like gravity, as much as you push against it will just push back. It's called Equality and it was invented by men and it's a good thing. Equality means that men now don't always pull the short straw. Equality means that now and again if you're a bit strapped, your missus feels obliged to get a round in. Or if you're at work

215

and the old sciatica is playing up, you're well in your rights to ask your female colleague (as they are now referred to) to hump that heavy box up the stairs (though Equality also means a passing remark about her backside as it ascends the stairs is out of the question: one step forward, two steps back as it were). Of course it hasn't always been this fair. Before Equality had been invented, it was all a bit too one-sided, men had to do all the work while women stayed at home, normally, usually, most of the time.

And the future?

There's still a lot of work to do, there's a few small changes that can be implemented that can make this world a fairer place. Just look at shopping, if the advertisements weren't always about how stupid men are, men might believe them and buy the products. And if air freshener cans weren't pink men might use them after they have been to the toilet... even after six months into the relationship. (Mind you, if my stack of *AutoTraders* ended up smelling of pine forests there'd be a row and no mistake.)

I said, 'Oi!'

NIGHTSWHENPEOPLEWHODON'T USUALLYGOTOTHEPUBGOTOTHEPUB

If I'm honest trade's been pretty slow since I started asking people to lay down a deposit for their pint glass. It probably wasn't the best move, and five pounds is a bit steep, but I'm standing by my guns. And after all, theft is theft. However there are nights in the Landlord's diary that he can be guaranteed to make a killing. This phenomenon is known as the 'Nightswhenpeoplewhodon'tusuallygotothepubgoto thepub'.

Of course it sticks in my craw to have to rely on these part-time drinkers, these fair-weather friends, these temporary alcoholics, these lightweight, semi-serious, *Guardian* reading booze phantoms, but so be it, I've got overheads. So, here's your Common Sense guide to the three most lucrative Nightswhenpeoplewhodon't usuallygotothepubgotothepub.

NEW YEAR'S EVE

New Year's Eve. The ultimate challenge on the publican's calendar. The Becher's Brook, if you like. Everest. The South Pole.

The honours board at the Honourable Order of Publicans is studded with the names of the fallen, those who were tested and found wanting. At the hanging up of the towels, at the unplugging of the fruit machines, we will remember them.

New Year's Eve, you see, is the ultimate Night When People Who Don't Usually Go To The Pub Go To The Pub. (See *ST PATRICK'S DAY, VALENTINE'S DAY.*)

Now, if Christmas is a time for family, then New Year's Eve is the time for friends. This is where the pub comes in, as no one wants to hold a party at their own place bang after Christmas, do they? You have to clear up all the Christmas mess, then let your mates in

One more year.

to make a whole new mess. Much easier to let the Christmas mess linger around till mid-Feb, and let all your mates go and be sick down the local, that's the thinking. And there's always the worry that your mates will smash up all your presents or nick something.

Long story short, it's a bonanza at the tills for your publican, provided he can handle the pressure. At first it will seem like any busy night. Bit of a press at the bar, bit of a queue building up at the ladies bogs, but nothing you can't handle. You move around behind your staff, offering a word of encouragement here, a pre-opened mixer there.

As you head towards the witching hour, though, things begin to get a bit mental. You pass a threshold when all the programmes on the telly are coming live from the bank of the Thames, for some reason, and are presented by the blokes who do the DIY shows during the day. The only exception to this is a Jools Holland show with the word 'hootenanny' in the title. All across the land homes are emptying as punters flee willy-nilly to their local pubs.

218

You look out, and as far as the eye can see there are sweating faces and fists waving tenners at you. This is the testing time. This is the time when grown men are broken.

What I find is that the training kicks in and I enter a state of grace. Everything seems to happen in slow motion. I'm like Michael Schumacher (although not in certain important respects) thinking two corners ahead. That bloke coming through the door now, he'll want two pints, two glasses of white wine, he'll be at the bar in about four minutes. Pull the pints, pour the wine, so what if I'm wrong, someone else'll have 'em. Reach for the nuts, don't have to look, I know exactly where they are. Totting up as I go, just get in the right ballpark, that's the thing, no-one checks their change, it's New Year's Eve. Ignore the regulars, serve the new faces, they're the ones who might go somewhere else next year. Pints for the fellas, glasses of wine/fruit-based drinks for the ladies, pints for the fellas, who's next please? Bring it on.

Before I know it, everyone's counting down and then trying to stumble through *Auld Lang Syne,* and I've made it through one more time. One more year.

And the memory of that, that triumphant personal glow, that has to keep me warm through January, that flu-blasted month of money-all-spent, Christmas tree bonfires, and no cheer whatsoever. Where are all those happy sweating faces then, eh? Not down the pub, that's where. Not shoving their hard-earned into my fist and slinging winter warmer down their necks. Bloody part-timers...

VALENTINE'S DAY

Six weeks after New Year's, which is the optimum time it takes to patch things up with your girlfriend who caught you snogging her best friend on New Year's Eve (you wish), comes Valentine's Day. This is not just a night for making an anonymous move on the girl at work who you once caught looking at you while you were doing the photocopying. It's not just a night for young couples to gaze dreamily and with increasingly poor focus into each other's eyes.

This is another one of those Nightswhenpeoplewhodon'tusually gotothepubgotothepub.

(See *NEW YEAR'S EVE, ST PATRICK'S DAY.*)

It's not quite the bonanza we get on New Year's Eve, not by a long chalk. Then people seem to be operating on the principle that there is an annual quota of beer to be drunk, and this is the last opportunity to meet their yearly target. On Valentine's, people, by and large, have other things on their mind. Your Valentine's couple comes in, but they're not settling in for a lucrative evening's drinking, oh no. They've come to the pub 'for a quick half' before heading out to the flicks, or for a romantic evening for two at *Bella Pasta.* And even if they do decide to spend the whole evening on the premises, chances are the fella is watching his intake, because he reckons he's on a promise just as long as he doesn't lose focus and start talking about football or motors instead of faking up some chat about 'his feelings', or worse still 'hers'.

No, the little of bit extra custom you can get from Valentine's couples is hardly going to make much of a blip on your pub radar. Maybe you can dummy 'em with a special offer – stick a pink paper heart on the pump and call it 'Love Beer' for the night, something like that. But the real surge is coming later in the evening. Because Valentine's is the night of the year that flushes out your solitary drinker like rabbits out of a warren after they've sent in the ferret, or wasps fleeing a paraffin-soaked nest. He's got no date, he's received no cards, he's lonely, he's unloved, he fancies a beer, and then he fancies

another nine. It feels like quite a quiet night, in some ways, because none of them are talking, and if you don't notice the odd sob there might be only the noise of the telly to distract you, but check your takings at the end of the night and you've done all right, don't you worry about that. Just as long as you haven't drunk it all away yourself thinking about how your wife ran off with a Frenchman. Thanks for bringing that up again.

He ordered red wine because he's someonewhodoesn'tgodownthepub

Abi 0777 550 6249 xx

ST PATRICK'S DAY

Ah the craic is mighty, ah the craic is good. So we're told. However, what this craic actually is has never been made clear to me. The craic, it would seem, is an exclusively Irish way to enjoy yourself that no Britonman can ever hope to understand. Nonetheless, we all seem desperate to give it a try, which is what makes St Patrick's Day another Nightswhenpeoplewho don'tusuallygotothepubgotothepub (see *VALENTINE'S DAY, NEW YEAR'S EVE*).

St Patrick's Day has the incredible transformative power of making Irishmen of us all – well, some of us anyway – suddenly out of nowhere the utterly 100% cockney bloke you were talking to starts to say: 'So it does, so it does...' and the urge to slap him rises in your gut and you have to walk away and spend the evening grinding your teeth.

It makes my blood boil, and it just makes me wonder what it is exactly they've got that we haven't got. After all, venture across the Irish Sea (if you must) and you will discover that drinking there takes very much the same form as here. People drinking pints of beer in pubs, and not necessarily that black stuff either (despite what they say in those Irish Tourist Board ads). Nothing peculiar about that. But let them get a whiff of an Englishman and what happens? They become twiddling diddling lepre-cocks,[90] that's what. Suddenly *they* know how to enjoy themselves in a mysterious way that we can never understand, and English hands feel clumsy as they clutch their pints of brackish black sludge.

[90] I thought of this, if you want to use it, you can pay me.

There will be those who say, well, the English should celebrate St George's Day and that'd show them. But the problem with that is what would we do? Have a few like any other day in the pub in England? There's no funny beer associated with it and St George is a fairy tale for kids. We don't have a national costume, and we can't all go around in suits of armour like St George, even one day a year. It's just not practical. Mind you, the St Patrick's Day costume seems to consist of a green plastic bowler hat – whatever you do my sweet Celtic friends, don't sell yourselves, your culture, your history and traditions short.

Truth be told the real reason that the English have never celebrated St George's Day is because we know who we are, always have done always will, and it doesn't require a bunch of traditions made up far more recently than anyone would care to admit to make us feel better about ourselves (yes, you in the kilt watching *Braveheart*).

The craic is mighty.

Let's look at the black stuff itself. It's not as though all these part-time Paddies are necking the stuff the other 364 days of the year, is it? Of course not. And let's not forget that it is in fact a British drink, owned by a British company. Furthermore,[91] no one likes it anyway. It's disgusting engine oil, a 48,000 mile service in a cup. The idea of the black stuff came from brewing burned barley. Well OK, but you wouldn't eat eight slices of burnt

---

[91] Never used that word before.

toast regardless of how traditional it was would you? Do you know how they get the white head? It's nitrogen, the same thing used in light bulbs and the manufacture of liquid explosives. Mmmm, fancy a pint?

Not to mention the fact that it takes at least seven minutes to pour, and in really Irish places the froth is cheerfully adorned with the devil's symbol, comprising three linked sixes, to make you sorry you asked for it.

And anyway, it wouldn't surprise me if the whole thing was a gag: 'Here let's make some truly disgusting beer – black too, urgh! – and see if the Irish fall for it!' And they did. The trouble is, the gag has back-fired, we've forgotten about the prank and we've started drinking it again once a year religiously wearing a tall black furry hat with a buckle on it, underneath some green bunting whilst overplaying that one Pogues song we know, you know the Christmassy one. Christ we've blown it.

See you next year, you twiddly-diddly so-it-is so-it-is black-sludge-swilling green-plastic-bowler-hat-wearing ginger-beard-sporting part-time time-wasters, you. To be sure.

Frankly I have no time for the people I only see on these nights and if I didn't owe Steve so much money after that three day Pokerthon when we shut the pub for a whole bank holiday weekend, I'd rather they didn't bother coming in.

FOREVER IN YOUR NATIONAL DEBT

Here's a Pub Fact for you: apparently as a Nation, Great Britain, clue's in the name, we're in debt for many, many, many, many billions of quid. Borrowed on your and my behalf, as a Country we owe something like 35 billion big ones, which means pal, you and I are down about seven grand each.

Seven grand! Think of the holiday we could all go on, prescribed on the NHS or whatever if they hadn't spent it already. So, what I want to know is: what the bloody hell did we spend it on? Fair enough if we'd have gone out and bought a huge Plasma screen the size of a football pitch or we'd extended the place a bit, perhaps a carvery on the side of Norfolk, one with baskets for the bread and those little blister-packs of butter on a tray by the cutlery. Or even a war on France, that would be okay. Imagine what we could do to the French with 35 billion quid's worth of military hardware...sorry I drifted off there, the thought of the Eiffel Tower

 melting as a result of a giant orbiting diamond-powered laser with a Union Jack on it was irresistible. But it looks a lot like we just borrowed a load of money and pissed it up the wall.

That's more money being pissed up the wall

Thing is we've all been there. The way that money can just evaporate from your wallet on a Friday night is something we're all familiar with, and sometimes you just have to have that new TV, but to mislay 35 billion squids seems somewhat slack. If I'd been that careless with my till the brewery would have my guts, I'd never work again, I'd be drummed out of the business and probably only find my way back into the trade by working for my brother at his wine bar, the Judas. What I'm saying is that tatty red square briefcase the Chancellor of the Exchequer carries around is empty, I tell you, there's nothing in it, and there's nothing in his pockets either. And seeing what we owe, it's little wonder we can't afford a nice new one for him.

There is a possibility that we whacked up a load on our tab fighting the Second World War (you'd think they would have learnt their lesson the first time round, but oh no). But if that was that, then the **Germans** would be paying it back seeing as they started it.[93] Either that or a discount on Beemers. But that's not the case, so what else could it be?

This is what I think happened: Gordon Brown is sat in 11 Downing Street one afternoon, not a lot on, watching *World At War* Day on UKGBTV History 3 when he fell for one of those ads: 'As long you're over eighteen and in full-time employment, you can borrow anything from five thousand to thirty-five billion pounds, no medical, credit check!' And he looks around the flat and he thinks you know those curtains are a bit drab and the next thing you know he's picked up the phone and borrowed 35 billion no questions asked, using everyone in the country's names to borrow seven grand apiece, consolidating all our outgoings into

[93] They did.

one easy-to-manage national debt. And it has to be said, the notion that we as a nation owe Carol Vorderman 35 billion quid scares me witless, especially as she probably knows the square root of 35 billion and can do the interest calculations in her head without moving her lips the brainy cow. Still you would, wouldn't you? It's been a year.

However there is a bright side, and it's this. If we really can't remember what we spent it on, then it must have been a fabulous night. Cheers!

two world wars +
unnecessary
colleges² x
arts centres +
4X³ single mums
= £35 billion

WHAT'S WRONG WITH THE BRITISH BEACH HOLIDAY?

I can never understand why people would want to go abroad for their holiday. The idea of having to travel for four and a half hours just to get to a country full of Spanish people sounds terrible and holidays are supposed to be fun, aren't they? Some of my regulars, though, they swear by the holiday abroad.

'You should try it,' they say. 'We went to Fuertemolinos and it was great. There was an English pub where you could have a full fried breakfast and watch Sky Sports all day!'

Heat magazine: SPF 27.

Well, I can do that here thank you very much, without cramming myself into a plane with dozens of bright red sweaty lobster people in sombreros clutching souvenir basketwork donkeys and small children.

'But the weather was so hot it was fabulous!' they say, and I point out to them that every year it gets hotter and hotter here, thanks to the beauty of Global Warming, and so every year the prospect of a foreign holiday gets less and less appealing. Think it Through. That's just Common Sense.

'Well,' they say, still not giving it up, 'what about the food, then, the food is fantastic!'

See here's the thing. When I eat a beefburger I want to know it's made from cattle that's been properly processed, not chased around a dustbowl by a team of blokes in fancy dress till it drops dead of exhaustion, in a feeble attempt to impress women with moustaches.

'A change is as good as a rest,' they say.

'All right,' I say. 'I'll have a rest.'

There's nothing wrong with a proper British beach holiday, in fact there's nothing better to recharge the old batteries. A crate of Stella, nicely warmed in the boot of the car, some curling sandwiches that you eat begrudgingly because the kids next to you have got Fish and Chips, and the family all sitting around on the dog blanket. Even now, if I think about it, the smell of that blanket comes back to me. Ah, Ramrod! He used to love the sea, his little eyes used to light up...

I loved my boyhood holidays, every summer we'd all get in the car and go down to Margate. We couldn't afford to stay there, obviously, hotels were too expensive even back then and Dad wouldn't stay in a B&B because he claimed to be allergic to candlewick coverlets, so we used to travel back and forward every day for two weeks. I loved that bit of the holiday, although I always put on a stone and a half in that fortnight with all the travel sweets I got through and surprisingly I never did work out what made them travel sweets as opposed to normal sweets.

Mum always used to go on and on at my dad about all the driving backwards and forwards to Margate and back until one year we borrowed a bloke's caravan, which was great. It meant that Mum and me and my brother got to have a kip while my dad drove us up and down the A2 every day. He wasn't going to pay for a camp site, he was far too tight. He used to park up at a bus stop

on the seafront and put a bit of cardboard box with 'Gone For PETRIL' written on it in the window. Worked a treat. Wonderful days.

We had such a laugh one year, the old man fell asleep in the dinghy and floated out to sea. The coastguard had to rescue him using the winch and the helicopter. He looked so stupid and humiliated, it was brilliant. I haven't got any photos I'm afraid as Dad lost the camera (along with my Subbuteo set) in a game of poker. I did draw a picture of him just before the helicopter got involved though. I was too busy pointing and laughing to draw anything during the actual rescue.

The funny thing was he was absolutely petrified, and it turned out it wasn't the drowning he was scared of, it was washing up in France in only his swimming trunks (which would terrify anyone normal). As the helicopter pilot said, he needn't have got so worried. The current would have taken him to Norway.

There was that time when my dad lost it while watching the **Punch and Judy** on the beach. He wasn't even supposed to be watching it, it was meant to be kids only, but he'd had a few and so the other mums and dads pretended they didn't mind. Anyway, my mum had been going on and on and on at him all morning about why wasn't there a decent chippy and how the caravan smelled of piss even before we'd been in there, and when Judy came on and started having a pop at Mister Punch, suddenly Dad leapt to his feet, threw himself at the little red and white kiosk, grabbed hold of Judy and tried to throttle her. And all the kids were cheering, and a couple of the other dads came and tried to pull him away, and Mister Punch was going mad, headbutting him in the eye, shouting:

231

'Naughty! Naughty! Naughty!' That was the end of that holiday, and the end of the show, too, because the Punch and Judy man had to go to hospital to get his wrist put in plaster. Happy days...

Yes, give me the British Beach Holiday every time. You don't need a passport, which is obviously a plus when you are deceased for tax purposes. You can make yourself understood without shouting and pointing. You can spend your British pounds and pence even though you are on holiday. You can buy sticks of rock with the name of the place you've been to written all the way through the middle, made by skilled craftsmen using ancient skills that are only practised in this country. You can buy an ice cream that is a rectangular slab of Cornish dairy stuck in a rectangular cornet. Don't have them abroad, do they? Back off Brussels! And even if you find yourself swimming around in effluent, at least it's *British* effluent.

PUB QUIZ CRIB SHEET (3) – THE NUMBER ONE HITS OF ABBA

Whether you, reader, are a pub landlord working up a quiz for quiz night, or a punter hoping to score a free pint and a couple of B&Q vouchers, you could do much much worse than familiarising yourself with this list.

ABBA, the girl-boy-boy-girl Swedish supergroup, captivated the music world in the Seventies by getting off with each other, splitting up again, getting back together again, breaking up again, and charting their raw emotional roller-coaster lives in song.

After wiping the floor with Olivia Newton John – who was Australian, and should really therefore have been competing in the qualifying competition for Oceaniavision against Kiri te Kanawa and Rolf Harris – at the 1974 *Eurovision Song Contest* in Brighton, the lovable not-particularly-mop-topped fab foursome went on to have hit after hit.

Nine of them got to number one, which is a good effort, but not as many as pretty boy roadgang escapees Westlife. Mind you, if you find yourself facing a pub quiz round about Westlife hits just write down a list of any songs you can think of at random and chances are you'll stumble across a couple that they've ripped off before too long.

Fifty percent eye candy. Fifty per cent songwriting.

CRIB SHEET No. 1

TOPIC Abba Number ones

1. **Waterloo** — This was the song that won Eurovision, a bouncy ditty likening the moment of falling in love to the defeat of Napoleon. Which is a bit of a stretch however you look at it, and not a move calculated to bring in the votes of the French jury. The Prussians loved it, though.

2. **Mamma Mia** — Despite the fact that Eurovision was in the bag, they still felt the need to suck up to the Italians for some reason. Baffling.

3. **Fernando** — Now they're schmoozing the Spanish. They had no shame. Bjorn and Benny return to their hit formula of writing songs about ancient conflicts, with this atmospheric number about the Spanish Civil War. No one else was doing them, then or since – can't think why...

4. **Dancing Queen** — One of only two songs ever written – the other being Car Wash by Rose Royce – that is absolutely guaranteed to get everyone onto the dance floor in your function room, even if it's a wedding where everyone hates each other.

5. **Knowing Me, Knowing you** — The various relationships in the group going through a bit of a rocky patch, clearly. No more carefree laughter. Being European, though, they couldn't keep a lid on it all, and the punters loved them for it.

6.  **The Name of the Game** — Now they're getting suspicious of one another. Who's trying to pull a fast one, here? That Hootenanny Singers LP was mine, I bought it before you even moved in. And I'm keeping the cat.

7. **Take a Chance on me** — The reason everybody likes this one – sure, the rhythm is catchy, and it has a nice tune – but everyone knew that the two couples in the group had split up, and in this song it sounds like the two girls are suggesting swapsies. Well, they are Swedish...

8. **The Winner takes it all** — By this time the blonde bird was all upset and on her own, while the other one, the one with maroon hair, was laughing it up with both the blokes. Which doesn't really seem fair. On the other hand, though, it might have made a better video...

9. **Super Trouper** — Bjorn and Benny are back on familiar ground here, as the title clearly refers to some sort of cavalry action. Not entirely sure what is going on, although there is a mention of Glasgow in there somewhere, so I'm thinking maybe Bannockburn...?

CRIB SHEET No. 2

TOPIC Abba Number twos

Of course Abba didn't only have number ones,
they also had a healthy smattering of number twos.

These didn't make it to the top spot:

1. Ring Ring — Wrong wrong...

2. I do, I do, I do, I do, I do — It didn't, it didn't, it didn't, it didn't, it didn't.

3. Money, money, money — Just not as much of it as you were hoping for.

4. Gimme, gimme, gimme — See what's happening here, lads? People don't like the ones with the repetitive titles. Learn your lesson. Move on.

5. Voulez Vous — Told you. And you'd already blown it with the French by having a dig at Napoleon, and there was no coming back from that.

6. One of Us — That's how many people bought it.

7. Under Attack — It was your reputation as a hit factory that was under attack by this time.

8. Thankyou for the Music — ...and goodnight.

MEN CAN ONLY THINK OF ONE THING AT A TIME

Here is a criticism that is aimed at men all too often – we can only ever think of one thing at a time, that men have one-track minds, that unlike women we can only concentrate on one task at one time and then move onto the next one...whereas women can juggle at least four or five mental concepts at once. That's great, that's fine. But if I'm flying a fighter bomber over Iraq trying to lock my missiles onto a target I don't want to be wondering about the merits of the cold wash cycle, which eyeliner to wear and whether water retention counts as weight gain. It's Common Sense. (See *MULTI-ASKING.*)

MULTI-ASKING

This is one of those topics that comes up again and again when folks compare men and women. Apparently women are better at multi-asking than men, always asking them to do lots and lots of things, giving them lists even, asking them to do new things when the man in question has yet to finish the nineteen other thing she has been asked to do. And you know what – this is indeed something that women are better at than men, mainly because we dare not ask them to do anything (other than all the stuff they ought to be doing and agreed to do when they married you).

THE BRITISH JURY SYSTEM – NOT ALL IT'S CRACKED UP TO BE

The British jury system is the cornerstone of justice that has been copied all over the world, even in places where the very idea of law and order is just that, a long forgotten idea, whispered in awed, hushed tones. You know…places like Portsmouth.

Anyway, the jury system operates around a simple principle. You make your case in front of 'twelve good men and true', and they put their heads together and decide your fate. Once upon a time this would have been deeply fair and sensible, in fact it would seem to be the very essence of justice, wouldn't it? But nowadays it's all gone to pot, and Common Sense tells us why.

It's because if you've got half a brain, or an even halfway interesting or important job, you can wriggle out of it, which means that juries nowadays are inevitably made up of jokers, chancers, wasters, and people with too much time on their hands. In short a jury in this day and age is almost certainly padded with people who would otherwise be sat at home watching the *Jeremy Kyle Show*, or else phoning up the *Jeremy Kyle Show*, or else actually appearing on the *Jeremy Kyle Show*.

Originally the whole principle of trial by jury, which seems to have fallen by the wayside in recent years, is the one which said you had a right to be tried by a jury of your peers. So if you were a baron, you had the right to be tried by twelve other barons, who would be bound to see your point of view if you'd stabbed a serf or something. Needless to say it was the barons that came up with this system and fair play to 'em, they were in charge at the time.

So taking this into account, it's clear that twelve inbred I-married-my mother-in-law Jeremy Kyle fans may not be the people you want to end up in front of when the scratchings hit the fan, or in my case the deep-fat fryer shorts itself because it's caked in filth and explodes in a shower of seven-year-old fat all over a seventeen-year-old working for less than the minimum wage.[94] He went up like a human candle and sputtered away slowly for just under quarter of an hour. Far better would be twelve other publicans who would understand the difference between culpable negligence and bad luck, who would know that getting round to cleaning one of those things is the last thing you're going to do now we've gone 24 hour opening (thanks a lot Tony) and that, frankly, deep-fat fryers have a mind of their own anyway, especially when they're caked in filth.

Same goes for anyone who's ended up throttling their wives after years of passive aggression and sniping. By rights he should make his case to twelve other blokes who've been through something similar, or maybe at a pinch ten of them and a couple of women with low self-esteem.[95] Of course there's a drawback here – by asking for a jury of blokes who'd done the

[94]Calling it minimum is simply optimistic.
[95]The bloke who invented self- esteem was terribly pleased with himself. The bloke who invented low self- esteem had discovered it years before but wasn't confident enough to tell anyone else. He felt terrible about it and blamed himself for the rest of his life. He went on to build on his earlier work and created self-loathing and despondency. The man who invented self-esteem then developed the whole idea of arrogance, and then made a major breakthrough and became insufferable.

same thing as you – i.e. murdered their wife – you're pretty much admitting to having done the same thing yourself. Just Thinking This Through, what you'd want to ask for is a jury of blokes who have been accused of throttling their wives but who got off.

Now you might say that some things are better about modern day justice. There's no longer much call for a return to Ordeal By Fire, for instance, and that thing of drowning witches to see if they'd drown just seems, well, stupid and obvious. And what about Legal Aid, eh? Surely that's a good thing? Well it is as long as you are able to get it. Fact is, as I discovered during the whole Health and Safety fiasco, that if you have decided not to exist for tax purposes then you don't actually qualify for Legal Aid. Mind you, they can't put you away, either, so it's swings and roundabouts, eh?

Justice. Not to scale

WHY IT'S TIME TO BRING BACK HANGING IF ONLY FOR THE SAKE OF THE ROPE INDUSTRY

Any self-respecting book of Common Sense is at some point going to arrive at the subject of hanging and why it's time to bring it back. There are many compelling arguments for bringing back hanging. Any parent out there will agree – it is a cast iron fact that the moment that you have children you instantly become more right-wing: just thank Christ himself that Hitler never had any children.

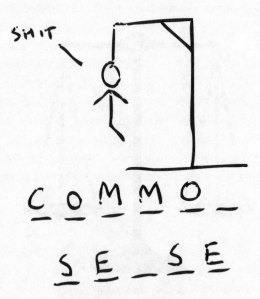

Two letters to go and only one
leg missing ... you do the maths.

But everyone must surely agree (and definitely when you're into your third pint) that there's something in it. Of course, it would be inevitable that innocent people might get hanged, but that just keeps the innocent on their toes doesn't it? And in this liberal soft-handed day and age it would be hard to agree on who you should hang. Those suicide bombers perhaps, but you can hardly hang them before they've done it as they're not suicide bombers until they've topped themselves, are they? So you can hardly do it afterwards, can you? That would just be demented.

The compelling argument for why we need to bring back hanging has more to do with economics than with crime rates or the evil that men do. Because since we got rid of hanging the British rope industry simply hasn't been the same. It's never recovered. The best rope you can get these days is that blue nylon stuff that you see round tramps' dogs' necks that is doubtless from China. British rope is one of the certainties upon which the British Empire was founded, holding together our noble sailing ships as they set off around the world in search of prime cricketing locations, but it has long since disappeared, you can't find it for love nor money. There's one or two people still making string at a loss, but there's no real way of knowing how much they produce, due to not being able to tell how long the pieces are.

Bringing back hanging, you see, would not only solve the problems of our rope import/export deficit, it would cure crime in a stroke, and not just the way you think. Because the main cause of crime a politician will tell you is unemployment,

unemployment causes crime,[96] that's what they say, and with all the rope factories shut down it's little wonder there are so many unemployed on our streets. And these unemployed loiter, cause crime, drift into serious crime, ultimately doing murders and the like. So, if the government brought back hanging, there'd be unprecedented demand for rope, and that blue nylon stuff has far too much stretch in it to do the job, so the government would have to set up a rope factory to meet the demand. Hence the unemployed are all off the streets in gainful employment, and down goes the crime rate. Problem solved.

Fig. 18 Find the better quality rope

[96]So why won't they lock up the unemployed? They refuse to think that one through.

Hang on a minute. I've started thinking this one through and it's beginning to do my head in. Setting up this rope factory would get people off the streets, reduce unemployment numbers, and thus reduce crime, fair enough. But that would therefore mean that there would be less call for rope. Which would mean the government would have to lay off people at the rope factory, they'd end up on the streets again driving up the crime numbers, meaning there's *more* call for rope all over again. What we have here is an eternal cycle – self-sustaining, economically viable, tough on crime, tough on the causes of crime and handy for towing caravans rather than tethering dogs.

PARLIAMENT

Politics is like a bird – you need a left wing and a right wing or you're going to fly around in circles or worse still just drop out of the sky. But when it comes to Parliament it's obvious that it's a British invention and no mistake. Because what we have here is a load of fat middle-aged men in ill-fitting suits shouting at each other about politics at four o'clock in the morning. It's a lock-in. And we're buying the drinks.

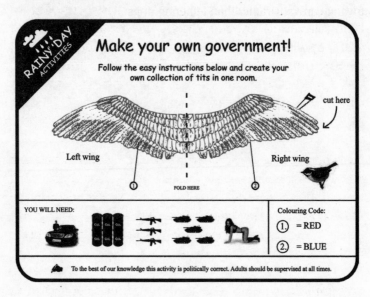

DOING THE BARE MINIMUM

QED [97]

[97] Latin abbreviation. I could translate it, but really can't be arsed.
(See 'BARE MINIMUM, THE, DOING'.)

The Crusades – Club 1130

The Crusades, or Club 1130 as I prefer to call it – they went abroad to the sunshine in their finest togs, smashed up the resorts, gave the locals flu and then sloped off having nicked loads of souvenirs – it's a noble and time-honoured tradition dating back to the 12th Century. All those Mediterranean countries still quake in their espadrilles at the prospect of being invaded by the Brits. The England football shirt awakens a long-dormant gene memory of being continually twatted by the Knights Templar, to the sound of a trombone playing the first eight bars of *The Great Escape* over and over again.

What a fabulous thing a Crusade must have been, eh? For a start, there is something terrific about the idea of the Church starting a war. That is a fabulous idea. You can see the monks now, can't you, eh? 'Come on over here if you think you're holy enough! Are you looking at my brother? Are you calling me a Albigesian heretic?! What do you mean you don't understand the idea of the Holy Trinity? Outside, come on!'

Back then the different religions didn't get together and wring their hands like *Guardian* readers about how they all believe in roughly the same thing but in different ways, and about how their religions simply offered different aspects of the same God: no, they got STUCK IN!!

The Crusades!! Richard the Lion Heart, Saladin with his bendy sword that cut through silk, what fantastic tales from the East! And what was best about it? There weren't articles in the *Guardian* whingeing on about how it was just a war for oil – they hadn't found it yet! It was a war in the Middle East for its own sake – how about that, eh? They don't make them like they used to, do they? Magic.

WRITE YOUR OWN ALAN BENNETT PLAY

Unlike some money-making schemes, this is not as difficult as it sounds like it's going to be. All you have to do is write down some normal conversation, and whenever you can, change the things the people are talking about to brand names.

Take this perfectly normal conversation phrase:

'I had a nice cup of tea and a biscuit.'

In your Alan Bennett play it becomes:

'I had a nice cup of Tetleys and a McVitie's chocolate hobnob.'

Or, to take a snatch of conversation from the pub only last evening:

'I had eighteen pints and a curry and puked me guts up on the carpet.'

In your Alan Bennett play this appears as:

'*I drank eighteen pints of Theakstons Old Peculiar, went for a Chicken Madras at the Taj Mahal, and then I puked me guts up on the Axminster.*'

See? Piece of Mr Kipling's Madeira. Keep doing this till you have about fifty pages. Now all you need to do is scribble Alan Bennett's name on it, and your own address for them to send the royalty cheques to, then stick it in an envelope and bung it off to the National Theatre. And if that doesn't work you could always try and flog it as a Victoria Wood sketch show.

WRITE YOURSELF YOUR OWN EARLY TOM CRUISE FILM

The world's smallest film star has one of the biggest wallets known to man – it seems flying around in model planes can make you a few bob. Bear in mind that Tom Thumb here gets paid $100 million a time – something like 50 million quid but not to be sniffed at – so there's bound to be some loose change knocking around.

All you need to do to get your mitts on some of this moolah is to write the kind of film Tom Cruise was in back when he started out, so if/when his career goes tits and he has to resort, as he inevitably will, to Plan A, you've already written the film for him.

Basically how these films work is this: Tom Cruise has to impress his dad for one reason or another: maybe his dad has died and Tom blames himself, maybe nothing he's ever done has been good enough for his dad, maybe his dad wants him to do something for a living that he doesn't want to do. You might want to include a scene where Tom shouts: 'No, you listen to me old man, this is something that I *have to do!*' The father doesn't

The world's best...
Fighter Pilot

248

actually need to turn up in the movie; his presence can hang over the whole thing, like Captain Mainwaring's wife.

So Tom finds himself a field of work in which he can be the best so he can prove himself and prove his dad wrong. This can be anything apart from Racing Car Driver (*Days of Thunder*), Fighter Pilot (*Top Gun*), Hustling Pool Player (*The Color of Money*), Barman (*Cocktail*), Sports Agent (*Jerry Maguire*), Mafia Lawyer (*The Firm*), Military Lawyer (*A Few Good Men*), Brother of Autistic Card Cheat (*Rain Man*) and Pimp (*Risky Business*), because he's already done those ones. You get the picture, but whatever you pick Tom will be trying to be the best at it. Obviously the less likely his dad is to approve of the job, whatever you decide it is, the better.

Tom gets a job in his chosen field, but soon learns from a mentor of some kind that talent isn't enough. You might want to include a scene where Tom is humbled by his mentor and has to realise that though he's good, *really* good, he's still got stuff to learn: he needs to listen if he wants to be the best of the best. After this stick in a bit where Tom goes running in the rain to shape up and get serious. A smarmy rival who is marginally better (for the time being) at what Tom is trying to be the best at usually goes well round about here, too.

And don't forget to bung in a bit of love interest somewhere, which can involve a hit from the Sixties songbook being either sung or

The world's best...
Pool Hustler

mimed to by Tom with the spontaneous backing of the entire population of a crowded bar/railway station/sports stadium.

Then comes the serious moment. This involves the mentor or possibly a trusting best mate dying or being harmed as a result of Tom doing something reckless, as he attempts to become the best. If you've got Tom being a gardener then perhaps his lawn mower spins out of control when he attempts a new cornering manoeuvre or maybe he's a window cleaner and reaches out too far for a sponge. I don't know, but what we have now is Tom's Crisis Of Confidence. He wanders around looking sad, wondering if his dad was right, and what his mentor (now deceased) would say/do. Maybe he splits up with the love interest here, on account of him being an obsessive monomaniac pill.

Then comes the bit at the end when Tom pulls himself together (more rain running here, to music) and faces a final testing task that he mustn't (and don't worry won't) get wrong. It turns out Tom is the best of the best at being the best at what he wants to be best at and his dad will realise that this is for the best. Tom now gets back together with his bird, and realises that there might be more to life than the thing he has decided to be the best of the best at. Don't overdo this as it can make the rest of the movie seem pointless.

Once you've written this up send it over to Tom Cruise c/o Hollywood with a covering letter saying that his early stuff was the best of the best at what he's the best at, which is playing someone who's the best of the best at being the best.[98]

[98] Surprisingly Tom wasn't in *Best*, a film about George Best, who was the best, God rest his soul we miss him in the trade.

The world's best... Brother of
Autistic Card Cheat

The world's best... Daytona driver

The world's best... Cocktail waiter

The world's best... Village Person,
erm I mean military lawyer

The world's best... multitasker

251

Common Sense
GET RICH QUICK
Scheme No. 0003

CREATE A CUT AND PASTE WEST END ROCK MUSICAL

These are sure-fire 100% dead cert winners no mistake. Most of the work's already been done, after all, and people who are desperate to fork out to go and see shows would much rather see songs they know already than risk hearing new ones which might be crap. All you need to find is a band who aren't around any more, who are sorely missed, and who have at least a dozen serviceable well-known songs that you can milk in a theatrical situation.

I would like to point out right now that I know nothing about the theatre, nothing whatsoever, in fact I hate it. In fact I'd go so far as to say that it isn't a job for a grown-up,[99] but this means I think I am in the perfect position to deliver something people will want to watch in large amounts: this show will not contain searing political comment, anything faintly allegorical about Iraq, anything with urchins, or people exploring their sexuality. For three hours with an interval.

---

[99] Let's face it – being an actor is not a job for grown-ups. Dressing up as a pirate, grow up. If you're ever in any doubt about this Common Sense fact, go watch some kids playing with dress- ups and you'll never be able to sit in a theatre again. 'There's no business like show-business' the old song goes, and this is in fact quite true, as all other businesses are for grown-ups. What it should say is: 'There's no off like show-off'. It might not fit the tune but it's no less true for that. They all say they're shy, don't they, actors, say it all the time, as they prance around in their stockings going: 'Look at me, look at me!'

So sort out your songs into an order, loudest one last, then join them together with a bit of a story. You will probably find you can get characters' names from words that are already in the songs, and place names, and some of the things that happen. Then get a couple of hundred kids straight out of theatre school, put them in stockings, and pay them peanuts, and you're almost ready to go.

Still to this day Simon Le Bon believes that he's right and it's everyone else that's out of tune.

OK, let's say you've decided to make a hit musical out of the songs of Duran Duran. First you grit your teeth, obviously, and tell yourself it's just for the money. And you can draw some comfort from the fact that it's very unlikely Simon Le Bon will be able to be in it himself, although he may want to swan into the first night party and ponce a few free seats or a box from time to time thereafter. Let the baby have his bottle.

So your main character is a girl whose name is Rio who's a model, right, and she and her mates, who are also models, i.e. Girls on Film, are being photographed dancing on some sand, which is what she likes to do, it's her hobby. All seems to be going fine, it's a routine modelling assignment, but hang on, who's that watching from over on the other side of the Rio

99 (cont.) And the next actor you hear saying it's really hard work should be manacled to forty other actors in a chain gang and made to bust rocks for ten years. It is apparently much more difficult to pretend to be a soldier than it is to be one. You're so creative – why don't you just make something, you great big make-up wearing, costume-flouncing, tight-sporting ponce? Still, I mustn't have a go, they do a lot of good work for charity.

253

Grande? It's a bunch of Wild Boys, what do they want? They look dangerous, surely they're not watching the girls with A View To A Kill? Well no, actually, but they haven't had their lunch, so they're really hungry. Hungry, you might say, as The Wolf (or wolves). Please please tell me now, they sing, is there somewhere we can eat? Come to my favourite caff, says Rio, it's called the Ordinary World.

The leader of the Wild Boys and lovely Rio get together, and she loves his eighties-style designer stubble: Don't shave it, she pleads, till the morning after. Anyway, turns out he's a keen amateur astronomer. Did you know, he remarks (in song), that there's a New Moon on Monday? Then down come some aliens in a spaceship, or something, and they're lost and they want to know what planet this is, so everyone tells them, or rather sings them, that this is Planet Earth, OK? Which is your big finish. Then you only need to work in The Reflex somehow – and good luck with that, because God alone knows what they were on about in that one – and give one of the characters a pet snake that gets off with another snake, and that's job done. See? It writes itself this stuff.

And the Wild Boys can all be in leather, and the models are all wearing stockings, so you're ticking all the boxes, aren't you?

Now we come to the bit where you really start coining it, because let's face it, the theatre's on its last legs thanks to DVDs and Play Station. You announce to the world that the only way you can get a lead actor for your show is by means of a prime-time phone-in show, which takes weeks and weeks and before you know it the whole thing's paid for itself before you even get to the theatre. Then you sit back and wait for the cash to start rolling in.

IT'S TRUE, MEN ARE AFTER JUST ONE THING

 There are lots of myths about men, most of which are true. But there are a few that are just that, myths. Hang on, if a myth is true then does that mean it's really a myth and that it's not true or when a myth is true, does this mean it's actually true in the sense of it not being a myth but more a fact? I've confused myself and I'm going to start again. Don't bother writing that down Gary.

Ladies, I think men are misunderstood and misunderstanding can lead to frustration. I think men are misunderstood by women because you think about us in the same way as you think about women. You search our behaviour and demeanour for little nuances, for clues to how we are feeling. You needn't bother. If there's something on our mind we don't say 'oh nothing', we say it straight. If we fancy someone we don't play with our hair (provided we have that option), we make advances, awkward clumsy and embarrassing advances, but advances all the same. And if we're angry we don't go shopping, we punch a hole in the wall. It's a lot easier being a bloke than a bird I reckon. I wouldn't be able to do and say the exact opposite of what I am feeling or thinking all the time, I'd slip up. I'd forget and go right ahead and accidentally say exactly what I was thinking. It must take years of practice to be that complicated.

255

Men are simpler than women; men want just one thing, the one thing that makes us feel good. One thing that makes us smile and one thing that colours all the decisions we make. This one thing? Happiness. That's all. We just like being happy. That's what motivates us, that's all, being happy. It's just so much easier than not being happy. Just look at how we deal with being unhappy. For example, if you women have a bad day you go and watch a sad film to make yourselves feel even worse and you cry it all out. Or you call your friends to talk about it and immerse yourselves in misery. Now to us men that just seems stupid, surely if you feel bad you want that bad feeling to go away. This is why, when men have had a bad day, we go down the pub and drink far too much and try and forget about it. Much more effective, surely? And if you're reading this and you disagree, then don't worry, it just means you're a woman.

THINGS YOU WILL ONLY EVER NEED TO KNOW IN A PUB QUIZ NO.1

Now as we come to the end of the book I feel I can share with you something very special, something that counts as privileged knowledge, passed on from publican to publican over the centuries, a rare and special fact, not a secret, no, but something that will change your life forever, something that will make you into a different person, a better one even. Something with which to astound your friends and confound your enemies. What it is is one of the two greatest mackerel-based pub quiz facts you'll ever hear.

Of course what I've got for you right now is the second greatest mackerel-based pub quiz fact you'll ever hear. Obviously the greatest mackerel- based pub quiz fact you'll ever hear is right at the end of the book. It wouldn't be Common Sense to put the second greatest mackerel-based pub quiz fact you'll ever hear before the greatest mackerel-based pub quiz fact you'll ever hear. Would it?

St John's Wood is the only tube station name which does not contain any of the letters from the word MACKEREL.

Of all the pub quiz facts this is probably the second greatest, and once learned it's never forgotten. Someone somewhere sat down and worked this out, that's what gets me. And when they extended the Jubilee Line and opened up the Docklands Light Railway they had a cold sweat moment where they thought: 'Christ! Never mind about improving the transport infrastructure of East London, that's completely fucked up my mackerel fact...! Oh no, phew, it's OK. And that rumour about them turning Bow Road and Bow Church into one single super-station called simply Bow...? Phew, just a rumour...!'

Anyway, it's a fact, there's no real doubt about it, but when would you ever use it, apart from in a quiz?

You're outside St John's Wood station, and you want to buy a piece of mackerel from a stone deaf street fishmonger. He doesn't have any mackerel on display, so you can't point at it, and neither of you has anything to write on, but you really want to know when he might next have some mackerel in.

You turn to the tube station sign, in the hope that you can use it to spell out what it is you want, but oh no! The tube station St John's Wood has none of the letters of the word MACKEREL in its name! What can you do? There's nothing for it but to take the deaf fishmonger with you down the Jubilee Line to Bond Street, change there to the Central Line and go one stop west to Marble Arch. Then you can use the sign there to point out the MAC and the EREL (using the E twice). Which just leaves you needing a K to make yourself understood, and you can point that out at Baker Street on the way back up to St John's Wood.

After all that, the fishmonger's probably going to say he isn't expecting any in until the weekend, and how many tube stations is it going to take for him to spell all that? No, don't use tube station names when you're buying fish. It just doesn't make sense.

#6 QUESTIONS BEST LEFT UNASKED

'Excuse me, Louis Walsh, when's the next Westlife album out?'

Music for Pussies and Chicks.

WHY IT'S TIME
SHAME
TO BRING BACK

**So join me in raising the shaming finger of shame and say
'Shame On You' to fifty deserving shame candidates:**

Airport staff who go on strike during the holidays! Go on your
strike during your own holiday! **SHAME ON YOU!**

All the women in the Daily Sport! **SHAME ON YOU!**

All the blokes who read the Daily Sport! **SHAME ON YOU! (Oh.)**

People who overfeed their dogs! **SHAME ON YOU!**

People who say the Americans never went to the moon!
SHAME ON YOU!

Moon landing denier Bart Sibrel. No wonder Buzz Aldrin punched
you out! **SHAME ON YOU!**

Bart Sibrel, shame on you for being punched out by a 72 year-old!
SHAME ON YOU!

Sven-Goran Erikson. It still hurts! **SHAME ON YOU!**

All the newspapers who told us that Sven was the saviour of
English football! **SHAME ON YOU!**

259

Shame on us for believing them…again and again! **SHAME ON YOU!**

Shame on me for still going on about it after all this time!
SHAME ON ME!

Louis Walsh: Westlife! Boyzone! **SHAME ON YOU!**

Australian pub chains! Bringing the idea of the pub back to the place it originally came from! **SHAME ON YOU!**

Wine bars! **SHAME ON YOU!**

People who read Harry Potter with the 'adult' covers! Shame on you! It's for kids! **GROW UP!**

People who think Pierce Brosnan was the best James Bond!
SHAME ON YOU! It's Connery.

Celebrities! Shame on you for thinking we're interested in you!
SHAME ON YOU!

Shame on that builder who ripped me off 4 years ago you know who you are! **SHAME ON YOU!**

You never bloody finished that extension and then disappeared claiming bankruptcy! **SHAME ON YOU!**

Heather Mills! **SHAME ON YOU!**

Shame on Elvis Presley for living in a thirty bedroom house and then bloody dying on the toilet! **SHAME ON YOU!**

Shame on the brewery for bringing in a graduate trainee as area manager! He's never pulled a pint in his life! **SHAME ON YOU!**

Shame on Diego Maradona for squandering the most incredible god given talents and ending up a fat chat show host (surely a fate worse than death?). **SHAME ON YOU!**

And shame on him for that cheating bastard Hand Of God cheating bastard cheating bastard goal. The cheating bastard.
SHAME ON YOU!

Shame on me forgetting the Hand of God thing momentarily! **SHAME ON ME!**

Hitler. For ruining that kind of moustache for everyone else. **SHAME ON YOU!**

And all the other stuff before you lot at the *Guardian* start complaining! **SHAME ON YOU!**

Those of you who bought the paperback! **SHAME ON YOU,** you tight bastards!

Downloaded it did you? Log off. Grow up. **SHAME ON YOU!**

Henri Paul. **SHAME ON YOU!** [100]

Shame on the bloke who sold me that Daimler Sovereign for £695, I just had a quote for repairs and the bastard's robbed me blind!
SHAME ON YOU!

Shame on the Labour government for bringing in the smoking ban, I've had to have my lawn re-turfed half a dozen times.
SHAME ON YOU!

All England football teams apart from the 1966 squad!
SHAME ON YOU!

You act all hyped up like you might win and then you always crash out in the quarters! **SHAME ON YOU!**

The 1966 World Cup Squad, shame on you for getting all our hopes and expectations way beyond reasonable limits!
SHAME ON YOU!

And for doing it on home turf! **SHAME ON YOU!**

It'll never happen again!! **SHAME ON YOU!**

Lawyers! With their bloody compromises! **SHAME ON YOU!**

---

[100] She was a candle in the wind.

Big Brother contestants! **SHAME ON YOU!**

People who write serious articles in posh newspapers about Big Brother! **SHAME ON YOU!**

Authors with writer's block. This book was knocked off in under a fortnight! Shame on you for sitting staring at the blank page, getting in a bate about it and feeling sorry for yourself! **SHAME ON YOU!**

Actors who say it's hard work! **SHAME ON YOU!**

It isn't! **SHAME ON YOU** for arguing!

Cyclists who go through red lights at pedestrian crossings! That light is not a suggestion, just 'cos you're doing your bit for the environment! **SHAME ON YOU!**

Anyone who thinks the Falklands War was wrong! **SHAME ON YOU!**

We won that on our own no help from no one else! Shame on you for doubting it! **SHAME ON YOU!**

Bottled water drinkers! Shame on you! Why did we invent the tap and sanitary hygiene? So you can drink water out of a foreign mountain? NO! **SHAME ON YOU!**

Shame on the Americans for inventing Thanksgiving which is essentially the same as Christmas but just before it therefore spoiling the whole thing. And you know what, we're not bothered about Thanksgiving, so could you kindly not put it in any more of your films and expect us to care! **SHAME ON YOU!**

The internet! **SHAME ON YOU!**

France! **SHAME ON YOU!**

LIFE'S GREATEST JOKES OF ALL

1. The way that as a teenager you think your dad is being an arsehole, when in fact the truth is it's you that's being an arsehole, of course you are, you're a teenager. And the greatest joke is, you're going to turn out just like him – an arsehole.

2. The more beer you drink the more dehydrated you will be in the morning. How is that possible?

3. The more beer you drink the more attractive the barmaid becomes at exactly the same rate – if not faster – as you become less attractive.

4. France.

AMERICA, AMERICANS

Don't get me started. They only asked for sixty thousand words. (See *BARE MINIMUM, THE, DOING*.)

☞ THE WAY THINGS ARE

No. 5: Timing Matters

Timing matters: like the way if King Cnut had sat down in his throne with the tide going out, the story would be very different. It's the way things are.

SUPER! ABSORBENT

THINGS YOU WILL ONLY EVER NEED TO KNOW IN A PUB QUIZ NO.2

Do you remember earlier on I showed you the second greatest mackerel-based pub quiz fact you'll ever hear? Yes I did. Keep up. Well as promised here is the greatest mackerel-based pub quiz fact you'll ever hear.

Obviously it comes after the second greatest mackerel-based pub quiz fact you'll ever hear otherwise it would be overshadowed and would not longer appear to be the greatest mackerel-based pub quiz fact you'll ever hear. So here it is...brace for impact... the greatest mackerel-based pub quiz fact you'll ever hear:

Another Mackerel

Ohio is the only American state which does not contain any of the letters from the word MACKEREL in its name.

It's a fact. Some loser sat down and worked it out. I don't know whether it was someone from the American Mackerel Marketing Board, trying to drum up some spurious publicity, or some hyper-patriotic American schoolkid with a fish fixation, but, whoever it was who stumbled across it, it is a bona fide fact.

But when would you ever *use* it, except in a quiz?

A friend comes up to you one day. Maybe not your best friend. Maybe someone you have been trying to keep at arm's length, because he seems to have an unhealthy enthusiasm for fish. Fish of all kinds, but particularly the mackerel. The mackerel is his favourite. So he's more of an acquaintance than a friend, because of the fish thing.

This acquaintance of yours is very excited. He has a plan. He tells you all about it one night in the pub over a beer. You are having the beer. He is having a home-made mackerel smoothie of some kind.

'Hey, you'll never guess what I'm going to do!' he cries. 'I am going to pay tribute to the mackerel, my favourite fish, by creating the world's largest acrostic. That's like a giant crossword, if you like.'

'I know what it is,' you say. 'There's no need to patronise me, fish boy.'

'OK,' he says. 'So this acrostic I'm going to do. All the across words are going to be the names of the states in the United States of America...'

'Hmmm,' you say. 'Interesting gimmick.'

'Yeah, but wait till you hear this,' your acquaintance jabbers excitedly. 'All the down words, the words going downwards, right...?'

'Right...'

'All the down words are going to be MACKEREL. That's right, MACKEREL. My absolute favourite of all the saltwater fish.'

'Well,' you say, sipping your pint thoughtfully. 'Good luck with that, you total mentalist.'

Seven months later you see him again. He has a wild staring look in his eye, and has grown a great long straggly beard. He looks like Neptune, the God of the Sea. He comes barreling up to you in the pub, with about an acre of paper in his arms.

'It's finished!' he cries. 'Finally! Seven months' work! I've hardly slept, I've hardly eaten, and now it's done. My life's work!'

Sure enough, he opens it all out, smooths out the creases, and tries to brush away a few rather odd-looking scaly stains, and there it is. A huge and intricately conceived acrostic. All the across words are the names of the states of the United States of America, and all the down words are the word MACKEREL, the name of the fish, his favourite fish.

'Congratulations,' you say. He looks at his watch, glances at the door, and says:

'Thanks. The bloke from the Guinness Book of Records is coming to check it out. This is the best thing that's ever happened to me.'

You look at the acrostic. You're impressed. You take a sip of your beer, and you say: 'Where's Ohio?'

'Ohio?'

'Yeah, Ohio. I can't see Ohio on there. You've only done forty-nine states. Plus D.C. of course, I can see what you've done, just stuck a D next to the C there. Where it says MACKEREL.'

Your acquaintance is staring crazily now at his huge acrostic, his eyes darting madly up and down, side to side.

'Ohio?!' he screams. 'That doesn't have any letters in common with MACKEREL, it doesn't concide at all! There's nowhere to put it! Nowhere at all!'

'That's a shame,' you say.

'All that work!' he raves, banging his head repeatedly on the pool table. 'All that time, wasted! Wasted!'

'Actually, I could have saved you the trouble,' you say. 'I happened to know that. I think I heard it in a pub quiz. It just slipped my mind for a moment when you were telling me about your plans seven months ago.'

He looks at you. A cold look. And he leaves. He goes down to the docks and throws himself headlong into the gutting machine on a mackerel trawler, shouting:

'O-HI-O!'.

It's his last word. And it's all your fault.

See, knowledge is worthless unless you know how to use it.

The same mackeral
on the return journey upstream.

ave you been paying attention?
re you bright and quick or are you thick and slow?
answers must come from this book, unless they're
t in here, and must not be fact checked on the
ody internet.

PUB QUIZ

£1 PER ENTRY

ROUND 1

GENERAL KNOWLEDGE

1) Who designed the Spitfire?

2) What is the name of my dog (deceased)?

3) What were my dear old dad's last words?

4) If we didn't have rules, where would we be?

5) If we didn't have hills, where would we be?

6) Where did the Vikings discover and not tell anyone?

7) Is there such a thing as ghosts?

8) How many is several?

9) What are eleven elevens?

10) What is a jumbuck?

11) What are the Zulus chanting in Zulu?

12) What is minus 1 times minus 1?

13) Who said 'This was their Finest Hour?'

14) Who was the best James Bond?

15) Who was the best Dr Who?

16) Which England legend had a pub?

17) Who won World War Two?

18) Who started it?

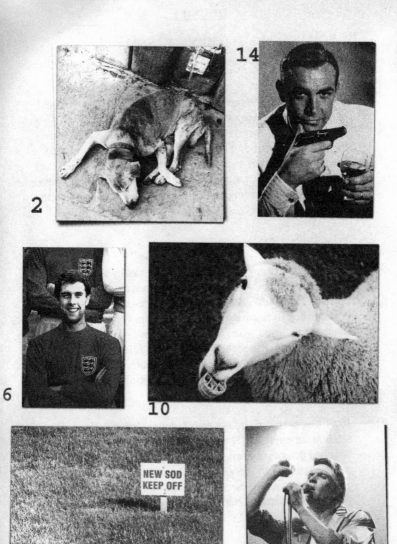

14

2

6

10

NEW SOD
KEEP OFF

28

19

ROUND 2:

MUSIC

19) Since the mid-18th century, tonal music has been increasingly composed of a 12-note chromatic scale in a system of equal temperament. Tonal music makes reference to 'scales' of notes selected as a series of steps from the chromatic scale. Most of these scales are of 5, 6 or 7 notes with the vast majority of tonal music pitches conforming to one of four specific seven-note scales: major, natural minor, melodic minor, and harmonic minor. But the yowling yelping lead singer of Duran Duran couldn't hit any of these even if he was driving a bus.

   What is his name?

20) The vocal cords are very complex: the airway at the level of the vocal cords is the glottis, and the opening between the cords is called the glottic chink. The size of the glottic chink is important in respiration and phonation. Open during inhalation, closed when holding one's breath, and held apart just a tiny bit for speech or singing; the folds are controlled via the vagus nerve. Not that the yowling yelping lead singer of Duran Duran can claim to have any control via his vagus nerve…but what is his name?

21) 1984 was predicted by novelist George Orwell to be a time of totalitarian oppression, where citizens had no privacy, the state watched your every private moment, and language was manipulated by the faceless state police as a way of controlling people. But one true horror that Orwell never predicted for the year of 1984 was the horrendous sound of Duran Duran. Who was their lead singer?

22) Who are the greatest band in the world?

23) What six CDs are on my jukebox?

24) What five ingredients make up a proper band?

ROUND 3:

BRITAIN AND CONSTITUENT PARTS

25. Who invented cricket?

26. Who discovered Australia?

27. Which country consists of England, Scotland, Wales and Northern Ireland?

28. What is article 1 of the Magna Carta?

29. Who won the World Cup in 1966?

30. For a bonus point who hasn't ever really got over and can't face the reality that we are indeed a second-rate footballing nation?

31. Where is Snowdonia?

32. Physics: Michael Faraday has often been referred to as the best experimentalist in the history of science. It was largely due to his efforts that electricity became viable for use in technology. The SI unit of capacitance, the farad, is named after him, as is the Faraday constant, the charge on a mole of electrons (about 96,485 coulombs). Faraday's law of induction states that a magnetic field changing in time creates a proportional electromotive force.

But where was he from?

33. The Scots haven't had a mention yet in this quiz.

But where are they from?

ANSWERS: HOW DID YOU DO?

GENERAL KNOWLEDGE:

1. Reginald Mitchell
2. Ramrod. I miss him that's all
3. 'I'm really bloated, I think I'll move onto the cider'
4. France
5. Holland
6. America
7. No
8. Four
9. One hundred and twenty one
10. A sheep
11. trans 'Get off my land'
12. One, not that it makes any sense or matters
13. Winston Churchill
14. Sean Connery
15. Tom Baker
16. Geoff Hurst
17. We did
18. They did

MUSIC

19. Simon Le Bon
20. Simon Le Bon
21. Simon Le Bon
22. Queen
23. Queen Greatest Hits 1, 2 and 3, Essential Sixties compilation, Wet Wet Wet Hits, U2's Achtung Baby
24. One bloke on the guitar, one on the drums, one playing the thick string on the bass and one other yelling.

BRITAIN AND CONSTITUENT PARTS:

25. The English
26. The British, which was fortunate for the people living there because they were lost
27. Britain
28. 'Please keep off the grass'
29. England
30. England
31. Wales
32. Britain
33. Scotland

ACKNOWLEDGMENTS

At the end of every decent book they have thank yous and all, so by having some thank yous here at the end of the book it's a way of telling you, the reader, that this is a decent book: Common Sense, that is. Also, it's not just Common Sense, it's good manners.

So, a big thanks to regular drinkers Mark and Chris, who sat around in the small hours arguing the finer points of Common Sense and making do with past-their-use-by-date dry roasted peanuts for sustenance.

Gary did a great job with the Polaroids, though, mate, if you ever burst in on me in the gents when I'm reading AutoTrader again, I'll gut you slowly.

The team at Unreal, who helped arrange the pictures on the page, which took some doing it has to be said, especially when you look at what passed for a manuscript at the end of the two week lock-in that produced this worthy tome.

The lads at The Caravan Gallery whose photos are truly top notch.

James, the youngster from the brewery, set all this up, mainly I think to get me to shut up about the carvery I haven't yet been provided with – really you deserve a pint mate, the next one's on me.

And finally a big pat on the back to Nick, the lad from Hodder who had to decipher all this and then get it into book form. Nice one mate: job's a good 'un.

PHOTO ACKNOWLEDGMENTS

AKG-Images: 33 (bottom), 35, 59, 62, 73, 74 (top), 74 (bottom), 76, 77, 78, 79, 147, 162, 271 (top right); Alamy: 12, 33 (left), 38 (top), 38 (bottom), 50, 51, 55, 56, 61, 81, 109, 115, 122, 151, 153, 154, 173, 190, 193; Anthony Blake Photo Library: 85; BBC Photo Library: 195, 197 (right); Ben Cook: 201; Bourne Gallery, Reigate/Bridgeman Art Library: 103; Corbis:116, 117, 120, 144, 146, 149, 171, 196, 216; Getty Images: 169, 178, 207, 212; The Kobal Collection/Columbia: 251; The Kobal Collection/MGM: 36; The Kobal Collection/Paramount: 34, 39, 248, 251 (centre left); The Kobal Collection/Touchstone: 249, 251 (top right); The Kobal Collection/United Artists: 251; PA Photos: 100, 180, 244, 271 (centre left); Redferns: 233; Rex Features: 143, 168, 194, 197 (left), 205, 227, 247, 253, 271 (bottom right); The Caravan Gallery (www.thecaravangallery.co.uk): 90, 150, 203, 225, 228, 230.

All other photography courtesy of unreal, we can't be bothered naming the pages they are on.

Illustrations by Mr Richard Horne.
Original hardback edition graphics and typography by unreal-uk.com, featuring MrBragg, Mat 'Copper Giles', Tabs, Simon, Kevanous, occasionally Brian, not Tim.
Paperback edition typeset and page layout by Craig Burgess

A

Abba 233-5
Aboriginal Australians 107
Agutter, Jenny 35 (in a heartbeat)
air-raid shelter, building 136 (not 'air-raid
  shelter, bombing of', that's in some
  German manual)
America 44, 48
American football 53
American Revolution 21
Amnesty International 161 (how did they
  get in here? Bloody do-gooders)
Andress, Ursula 79 (definitely)
Animal Rights 160, 161 (That's a page
  reference, not some sort of zoological
  version of Combat 18)
animals 43, 203-4
Antarctica 47
asthma flowchart 14
Australia 47
Australians (as bar staff, obviously) 47, 86-7
Austria 44 (Hitler was Austrian. And
  vegetarian. That's what I call a double
  whammy.)
Autotrader magazine 26, 27, 147, 215, 216

B

Bacchus 117
Bad Thinking 1
Baffin Island 49
Baird, John Logie 172-3
Baker, Hylda 195
Baker, Tom 80, 205, 206
bar snacks 126-8
bar staff 86-7
Barron Knights 17 (good but they're no
  Queen)
baseball 53
Battle of Britain (glorious skin of our teeth
  victory, on our own, no help from anyone
  else) 94, 95, 124
Battle of Britain, The (film) 34
BBC (British Broadcasting Corporation) 60-

61, 205, 207
  World Service 61
beach holiday, British 228-32
Bean, Sean 78
Beatles, the 15, 99 (good but they're no
  Queen)
beer gardens 90-91
Belgium 97
Bennett, Alan: write your own Alan Bennett
  play 246-7
Benz, Karl 31
Berry, Halle 79 (I'll delect her)
bitter 102
Blair, Tony 25
Blake, William: 'Jerusalem' 159
Blitz, the 24, 68
Boat Race, Oxford-Cambridge 57
Bond films 71-80
Bond, James Bond 71-80
bottle openers 103
bottled beer 101, 103, 175
boules 54, 59
Bowen, Jim 207
bread sticks 128
Bridge Too Far, A (film) 35
British character traits 19-25
  'the Blitz spirit' 24
  'British fair play' 19
  'Distinguished old age' 21
  'Everyone thinks in English' 22-4
  'Follow through' 20
  'The Great British sense of humour' 21
  'Mustn't grumble' 19-20
  'Never forgive, never forget' 25
  'Never say die' 22
  'Popularity' 25
  'Revolution? No thanks' 20-21
British folk tales 148-52
British Grand Prix (pro bri-tish gra-and
  pri-ks) 55
British Open 59-60
British thinking quiz 13-14
Brittas Empire, The (sitcom) 191, 194
Brosnan, Pete 78

Brown, Gordon (I never voted for him) 226

Brussels 121, 123

Buddha 116

Burton, Richard 36, 37

C

Caine, Michael 19, 33, 35, 162, 164, 165

Cam, Sidney 95

Canada (home of Canadians) 48-9

Carlyle, Robert 78

cars
  car conversations 26-9
  if your car falls into a river 138
  tubeless tyres 31

carveries 154-5

Casino Royale (film) 71, 74, 79

Chance in a Million (sitcom) 194

changing barrels 6, 86

Changing Rooms (TV programme, as opposed to the action of leaving one room and entering another) 173, 215

Channel Tunnel 97

character, British see British character traits

chefs 157-8

China 45

Christmas Island 46

Church of England 112-13

Churchill, Sir Winston 10, 124-5 (not as many references as Michael Caine, but more than Hitler if you include this one)

Cillit Bang (advert) 67

Cleese, John 162, 191, 192

Colombia 48

Common, Alf 168

Common, Ealing 7F 63

Common Sense (cover to cover, obviously)
  how does it affect me? 5
  jukebox 15-16
  knowledge 3
  thinking it through 4-5
  what is it? 2-3

Connery, Sean 35, 72-5, 78, 206

Construcciones Aeronáuticas SA 2.111s 34n

corkscrew 30, 103

Coulthard, David 27-8

Countdown (TV show) 61

Craig, Daniel 79

Craig, Wendy 197 (definitely his mum)

crisps 43, 104, 126, 127

Crouch, Peter 168

Cruise, Tom 37, 51, 142
  write your own early Tom Cruise film 248-51

Crusades 149, 150, 245-6

D

Dalton, Timothy 77

Dambusters, The (heavily dubbed film) 34

dartboards 89-90, 101, 104, 200

Darwin, Charles 47

daytime-television 215

Deal or No Deal (TV guessing game with that bloke from Noel's House Party)) 51, 52n

Dench, Dame Judi 77 Get off! She looks older than that?

Denmark 44

Descartes, René 81

Diamonds Are Forever (film) 75

Diana, Princess (candle in wind) 33

Dickinson, David 215

Die Another Day (film) 79

dips 128

Dirty Dozen (film and more than ropey TV series) 36

dogs in pubs 3

Dr Who 173
  the best Dr Who 80, 205-6

Drebbel, Cornelius Jacobszoon 30

drinking games 39, 162-5

Duran Duran 15, 32, 76, 253 Hang on why do they have more mentions than Queen?

E

Eagle Has Landed, The (film) 35, 36
East Anglia 97
Eastern Europe 44
Easton, Sheena 76 (try and stop me)
Eastwood, Clint 36-9
Edmonds, Noel 52n, 204*n*
education 63-4
EEC 122
El Cid 152
English Channel 97
English language 22-3, 42
equality 214-16 (We'll have it one day lads)
Escape to Victory (film) 34
Euro, the 121 (over my dead body)
Every Silver Lining (sitcom) 194

F

Faith in the Future (sitcom and proof of just
   how low the bar really is) 194
Falkland Islands (we won, on our own, no
   help from no one else) 47, 50
farming 119-23
Fawlty Towers (sitcom) 191
Ferguson, Sir Alex 168
feta cheese 128
films see movies
Fleming, Ian 79-80
Flynn, Errol 151, 152
Focke Wulf FW 190 fighter 95
folk tales, British 148-52
football
   coach, manager, pundit, pub 166-70
   pub quizzes 200-202, 207-9
Forbes, James 31
France, The 25, 43, 67, 70, 81, 97, 171, 263
   bowls 18
   bravery of ...
   language 23
   parks 18
   wine production 30
Frasier (sitcom) 192

French, Dawn 168 (why ever not?)
French Foreign Legion 61, 146
French Revolution 21
Fresh Fields (sitcom) 194
Freud, Sigmund 32
From Russia With Love (film) 73

G

Galapagos Islands 47
Ganesh 117
gastro-pubs 156-8, 174
gentlemen's clubs 175
George and the Dragon (sitcom) 196
Germany 11, 20, 24, 45, 124, 211 Hang
   on, where's the special font? They're
   obviously run out of Letra-set.
Germany
   folk music 37
   humour ...
   lack of humour 37
   language 23-4
   motor cars 31
getting your round in 88-9
glass washing machine 137
glasses, cleaning 6, 10
global warming 96-9, 183n, 229
Glorious Revolution (1688) 20
God (who is British) 31n, 49, 105-6, 108,
   116, 117, 145
gods, olde 198-9
Goldfinger (film) 73
Good Life, The (sitcom) 195
Grace and Favour (sitcom) 195
Grace Under Fire (sitcom) 195
graduate trainees 50-52
Grand National 58
Great Britain 42, 49 (clue's in the name)
Greenland 49
Greenpeace 159, 183
Greenwich Meantime 42
Guns of Navarone, The (film) 36

279

H

Hamish MacBeth (TV series) 78
hamster wheels 160-61 Why were you
    looking this up?
hanging, bringing back 240-43 When you
    could have been looking this up!
Hanley, Jenny 75
Harold, King 213
Hastings, Battle of 1066
Hawaii 47 (not a prequel to TV series
    Hawaii 50)
Hawker Hurricane 95
Hawkins, Jack 163
Heinkel He111s 34n
Henry VIII, King, I am I am 9-10
Henshall, Revd. Samuel 30
Heston, Charlton 149, 151, 152
Hill, Benny 21
Hill, Jimmy 167
history debunked 66-9
    quiz 70
history of the publican 6-10
Hitler, Adolf 24n, 88, 125, 240
Holder, Noddy 142
Holland 97
Holland, Jools 218
Holness, Bob 71, 75
Honourable Order of Publicans 6-10, 217
hoovering the house (One for the ladies,
    bless 'em) 137
Hopkins, Anthony 35
House That Jack Built, The (sitcom) 195
human beings 203-4
humour 21 So what is saying is that only
    one page of this book is funny. You still
    bought it though. Now who's laughing?
humus 128
Hurst, Geoff 169

I

Ice Cold in Alex (film) 35
Iceland 49
India 46-7

Industrial Revolution 19, 20
Inspector Morse (TV programme) 215
International Date Line 45
inventors, British 30-31
inventors, Australian
Ireland 43
Italian Job, The (film, the first one) 33
Italy 44
ITV 61 (without a doubt Britain's premier
    entertainment channel)

J

James, Sid 196
Jaws (Benchley) 108
Jeremy Kyle Show (TV show, Kilroy but
    harder, though looking at Kyle I expect
    he's against the Euro as well) 237
Jesus Christ 8, 9, 30n, 112-15, 190
John, King 16, 17, 149-50
Johnson, Dr Samuel 12
jukebox, Common Sense 15-16
jury system, British 237-9

K

Kant, Immanuel 193
Kelly's Heroes (film) 36
Kipling, Rudyard 62
Knights of the Round Table 9

L

lager 89, 102
Lake, Simon 30
Land of Hope and Gloria (sitcom) 196-7
landlords 6, 85-6, 168, 200
Last Supper 8, 9, 30n
Laura and Disorder (sitcom) 197
Laurel and Hardy 146
Lazenby, George 'Lucky' 74-5
Le Bon, Simon 'Lucky' 253
Lee, Christopher 76
left-handedness, as not normal 5 (Well it
    isn't)
life's greatest jokes 263

Litchfield, P.W. 31
lock-ins 88
Loose Women (TV programme, that is no
    way as good as it sounds, the fact that it's
    on at lunchtime should serve as a clue,
    but too many times now I've been lured
    in and left feeling stupid. Story of my life,
    it's been a year) 215
Lord's Test Match 57-8, 61
Lulu 15
Lumley, Joanna 75 (I don't care how old
    she is I would)
Lynam, Des 61

M

McCartney, Paul 76
Magna Carta 16-17
Mann's Best Friends (sitcom) 196
Maoris 107
Masons 7
maths - you'll never need it 65-6
men
    after one thing 255-6 (and you know, at
        least we have focus)
    one-track minds 236 (see what I
        mean?)
menus 154-6
Messerschmitt Bf109 95
Metro 183, 188
Mexico 48
Middle East 46
mild 102
milk 119-21
Mitchell, Reginald 94
Mohammed 117
Monaco Grand Prix (pro mon-aco grand
    pri-ks not as good as bri-ish) 55
Mongolia 45
Moonraker (film) 80
Moore, Roger 75-7, 78
Morecambe and Wise 61
Moses 109, 110
Mount, Peggy 196 (clue's in the name)
movies, top ten 32-5

Mr Tambourine Man 15
multi-asking 236 (If you only read one bit
    of this book read this)
music 15-16

N

nachos 128
Napoleon Bonaparte 25
National Debt 225-7
Neill, Terry 169
Nelson, Barry 71
Nelson's Column (sitcom) 196
New Year's Eve 217-19, 220
New Zealand 47
Newton John, Olivia 233
Newton, Sir Isaac 147
Niven, David 74
Noah's Ark 108
Normans 210-13
Not On Your Nellie (sitcom) 195
Nutt House, The (sitcom) 195

O

Oddie, Bill 50
off licences 176
Oliver, Jamie 24 see also Adolf Hitler
olives 127-8
On Her Majesty's Secret Service (film) 75
one-track minds 236
Open Golf Tournament 59-60
opening, 24 hour 25n
O'Sullivan, Richard 152
Oval Cricket Ground, London 58
ozone layer 99

P

Panama 48
Panorama (TV programme) 33
parallel parking 135
Parliament 244
peanuts 43, 51, 103, 126-7
pelota 54
periscope 30

Peru 48
Pharaoh Islands 49
Pink Floyd 63n (good but no Queen)
Pires, Robert 77
Pogues 224
Poland 45
pork scratchings 85, 86, 118, 126, 127
Portugal 43
post offices 176
practical advice
    build an air-raid shelter 136
    fell a tree 137
    hoover the house 137
    parallel park 135
    pull the perfect pint 131
    tying a tie 132-4
    use the glass washing machine 137
    what to do if your car falls into a river
        138
Prince Among Men, A (sitcom) 196
pub conversations (though let's be fair
    this book is made up entirely of pub
    conversations)
    cars 26-9
    quality of 4
pub names 91-2
pub quizzes 10
    Britain and constituent parts 273, 274
    British thinking 13-14
    football club nicknames 200-202
    general knowledge 270-71, 274
    history 70
    improving your chances 4
    mackerel-based pub quiz facts 256-8,
        264-8
    music 272, 274
    number one hits of Abba 233-5
    pub quiz (£1 per entry) 269-74
    Scottish football club nicknames 207-9
pub or wine bar? 84-93, 101-4, 126-8, 154-8,
    174-6
    bar snacks 126-8
    the bar staff 86-7 see also Australia
    a beer garden 90-91

blokes get their round in 88-9
check for pub basics 85
check what is on draught 102-4 (I said
    it was a book on common sense did
    I not?)
a dartboard 180 (no only joking it's on
    pages 89-90)
gastro-pubs 156-8, 174
the landlord 85-6
menus 154-6
other things to watch out for 174-6
the pub's name 91-2
regulars 87-8
publicans, history of 6-10
pulling pints 86, 103, 131
pumps 102, 103, 104
Punch and Judy (a combination that causes
    a sleepless night for Richard Madeley)
    231-2
Pyramids 8

Q

Queen 15, 63n
questions best left unasked 28, 52, 93, 104,
    170, 258
Quincy (television programme) 215
quizzes see pub quizzes

R

Ramsay, Gordon 169
'real' ale 102
recycling 99
Redford, Robert 35
regulars 87-8
religion 105-18
    beliefs 107-8
    the Bible 108-9
    Church of England 112-13
    creation 106-7
    God 31n, 49, 105-6, 108, 116, 117
    Jesus 8, 9, 30n, 112-15
    olde gods 198-9
    other religions 116-18

Ten Commandments 110-11
Robin Hood 16, 149-52
Robin's Nest (sitcom) 196
Rolls Royce Merlin engine 34*n*, 96
Roman's Empire (sitcom) 197
Romulus and Remus 152
Running Wild (sitcom) 197
Russian Revolution 21

S

St George's Day 223
St John's Wood 257-8
St Patrick's Day 222-4
Sartre, Jean Paul 171
S.A.S. 180
Schmeichel, Peter 170
Schumacher, Michael 140, 219
"Scott, Barry" (Neil Burgess) 67
Second World War (with no help from no
  one) 11, 13, 14, 20, 24, 25, 36, 38, 81, 226
Seinfeld (sitcom) 192
seismometer 31
Shakespeare, William 82-3
'Shame on You' candidates 259-62
Shankly, Bill 100
Sharpe, Lee 170
Sharpe (series) 78
shoes, number of 69 (that's how many she
  says she's got pal)
Simpsons, The (television animation series)
  67
sitcoms, top twenty 191-2, 194
Six Nations Rugby 60
Sky 6, 60
  Sports 118
Smoking Ban 91
snug bars 2
Sooty 61
Spain 43-4
Spanish Armada 25
Spitfires 34n, 94-6
sport 53-61
sports bars 175
Stalin, Josef 88

Stallone, Sylvester 34 (RECONSTRUCTION:
  "Go on mate, one last *Rocky* film" "no,
  no, really I couldn't" "Go on" "oh alright
  then")
stamps 31
'Stans, the 46
Starr, Ringo (Odds on favourite to be the
  last Beatle left) 99n
stiff upper lip 31, 34
Stonehenge 7-8
submarine 30
survival guide (when you're too drunk to
  go home) 180-89
  find water 181-2
  keep warm 183
  camouflage 184-5
  sleep 185-7
  home sweet home: get your story
    straight 188-9
sushi (Japanese for 'lazy chef') 157
Sweden 44
Switzerland 44

T

television 172-3, 175, 176
  daytime 215
Tell, William 152
That's Life (TV programme) 22
thinking it through 4-5
  he didn't think it through
    Number 1 12
    Number 2 62
    Number 3 81
    Number 4 100
    Number 5 147
    Number 6 153
    Number 7 171
    Number 8 190
    Number 9 193
Three Degrees 197 (correct temperature
  for storing alcopops, which doubtless
  where they got their name)
Thunderball (film) 73
tie-tying (not to be mistaken with hippy

pastime of tie-dying) 132-4
Titanic 10
toilets
    flushing toilet 31
    gents 63
    toilet paper 31
Tomorrow Never Dies (film) 79
Touchcloth (Torchwood) 206n
Tour de France 58-9
tree-felling 137
Tropic of Cancer 47
Turpin, Dick 151-2

tyres, tubeless 31

U

U2 16
UB 40

V

Valentine's Day 220-21
Venezuela 48
Vickers 95
Vikings 25
Vorderman, Carol (brainy cow, yet still...)
    227

W

Walkabout (film) 35 (Not to be mistake
    with Dom the Aussie barman's three day
    benders)
way things are, the 5, 96, 123, 189, 263
weddings 139-45
    mother-in-law 142-3, 145 (that's my
        mother-in-law trying to count to 10)
    personal experience is what counts
        141-2
    two kinds of wedding 140-41
    the vicar 144
Wembley 56-7

West End rock musical, create a cut and
    paste 252-4
Westlife 233
Wet Wet Wet 16
Where Eagles Dare (film) 32-3, 35, 36-8,
    67, 215
    drinking game 39
Wild Geese (film) 36
Wild Geese 2 (same film) 36
William the Conqueror 213
Williams, Robbie 94n One tiny mention in
    a footnote.
Wilson, Ray 167
Wimbledon 54-5, 61
wind turbines 159-60
wine bars see pub or wine bar?
Wogan, Terry 78
women: what women want 32
    (Surprisingly, edited to one page, but
    again, if you only read one part of
    this book read this, and the other bit I
    mentioned earlier)
Wood, Victoria 247 (suppose so)
work 177-9

Y

Yarwood, Mike 61
You Only Live Twice (film) 73
Yugoslavia 45

Z

Zulu (film) 19, 33
    British wearing red jackets see British fair
    play
    drinking game 162-5

Words that didn't make it into my index

The